PRIVATE COLLECTION OF THE TEACHINGS OF THE MASTERS

VOLUME II

Athena Hamilton

The Book Guild Ltd
Sussex, England

The Book Guild Ltd
25 High Street,
Lewes, Sussex

First published 1998
© Athena Hamilton, 1998
Set in Times
Typesetting by
Keyboard Services, Luton, Bedfordshire

Printed in Great Britain by
Bookcraft (Bath) Ltd, Avon

A catalogue record for this book is
available from the British Library

ISBN 1 85776 357 2

PRIVATE COLLECTION OF THE TEACHINGS OF THE MASTERS

VOLUME II

CONTENTS

INTRODUCTION

Volume I of the *Private Collection of the Teachings of the Masters* gave us messages of love, encouragement and wisdom from the angels, archangels, Ascended Masters and Supreme Universal Power.

This volume II continues these teachings, introduces us to new ideas and offers us guidance as we move towards the next millennium.

The fundamental alterations to our planet foreseen in Volume I are already in evidence through dramatic changes in our climate and ecosystem. This book provides invaluable guidance on how we can continue to adapt to our environment to meet the challenges that lie ahead. We need help if we are to develop our spiritual beingness and become less dependent on our physical form. Contained within these pages are messages of love and hope and the shared knowledge of those who have gone before us.

This book also expresses the experiences of the channellers and the instructions they have received for passing on their messages to others. Light Beings will be drawn towards the circle and will be warmly welcomed and encouraged to open their hearts and souls. A time of love, respect and enlightenment is almost upon us and our shared knowledge will help others nurture these qualities and pass on the teachings which have been so generously shared with us.

Quan Yin, Beautiful Bodhisattva of Compassion

Long Renowned in the Asian Countries of Vietnam, Mongolia, China, Japan, India and Tibet, to mention only a few, Quan Yin is more often referred to as the Goddess of Mercy.

We must understand that she is the only woman who has attained to the title of Bodhisattva. The word Bodhi is a generic term signifying 'The urge to wisdom, compassion and Enlightenment'.

Tradition has it that when Quan Yin was to be given the title of Enlightened One, Buddhist priests were so unaccustomed to granting the title to a female that they asked her if it would not be better if she die and ask to reincarnate as a male. Needless to say, Quan Yin refused.

In a poem quoted by John Blofield in his book entitled 'Bodhisattva of Compassion,' Shambala Press, Boston 1988, The Stanzas from page 105, he cites a poem translated from a Chinese master's rendering of the original Sanskrit made in the 3rd century AD which states:

> 'The echoes of her holy deeds
> Resound throughout the world.
> So vast and deep the vows she made
> When, after countless aeons
> Of serving hosts of perfect ones
> She voiced her pure desire
> To liberate afflicted beings.'

Quan Yin, the great Bodhisattva Mercy, as viewed from a statue dating from a
Mongolian era.

REMEMBERING TOGETHERNESS

Quan Yin

'I do treasure this moment my dear, dear Mary and it may seem to be only another one of these comings-together and a session of talking to one another, but this is an evening – a Sunday evening – and you are in my temple and I welcome you my dear. I have taken the opportunity of innovating something that you have not done before, for I am within you and your voice is my voice, your heart is my heart and your thoughts are my thoughts. It isn't seemingly very different from what it has been before but you may feel differently, you may feel a pressure upon your brow, you may feel that you are totally disconnected, which is true. We are not just experimenting my dear, but we are practising, for this is an occasion that will take on great momentum as you and I become accustomed to one another. It is that symbiosis that goes on between two living beings; I on my dimension and you on yours. It is sometimes limiting for us to do such a thing and it is not done often and certainly not without the permission of the most Almighty Father. I have been asked if this was possible for you and I to become more alike, that you may truly become my spokesperson and may address groups and those who are in trouble, those who are seeking for higher guidance and often do not know what they are looking for, but through the piercing eyes of the divine there is a way of knowing that their hearts are reaching out. There is perhaps a

1

memory of abandonment or a memory of a childhood pain, something that has been seen or witnessed that cannot be forgotten or erased and that is where the gift of enlightenment can be so precious, so that truly in your work you will touch those who come to you not knowing why or how or what was that simple statement that was made that seemed so profound and had such a far reaching effect and you are given the credit my dear, though you and I will know that it is our partnership, it is your devotion and your willingness and the offering of your gifts to serve Spirit that have made this possible.

I have looked for some time for a vehicle, someone who would represent me on this planet Earth and you have been chosen – not just because you made a sacred space for me, a temple, a meditation room if you will – but that you have filled it with your love. You have come at all moments and often at night in your sleep – without knowing – and you and I sat and spoke. We have been together and shared much, remembering past lives, our experiences together where you were sometimes the teacher and, at times, I was your guru. There is a familiarity that goes on between us like a knowingness and you are beginning to recognise the signs when I am present and when I am, perhaps, invading a space that is not mine, but I do know that you have given me permission on a higher level and that it is all right and in divine order.

So, as we become more acquainted with one another, there will be a period of growth here and growth is often painful. Do not be alarmed, my dear; you know and your heart and your soul know that this is only a temporary situation, that soon it will become so familiar and so "welcome", if I may say so, that you and I will rejoice in our hearts and we will be truly only one, joined together in Spirit and in our love for one another. This is something that is extremely powerful, for God does not give this permission easily and it is something you and I have worked very hard for: allowing one another the space to create in, allowing our individuality to be expressed separately, yet, when we come together, there is a such a blending. Can you imagine a wonderful painting with water-colours and how the colours flow when it is wanted, that the

2

water's edge will suddenly blend into the clouds or there may be a sharp line and next to it something very fluid?

Remember the Turner paintings that you admired so much in the Tate Gallery in London and how the splashes of colour came across so dramatically? Truly, Turner was seeing into the invisible, into the realm of Spirit where colour and light play upon surfaces, where they penetrate and where they stand out and where they erupt like a volcano and where there are pleasant, soft pastel colours, and then they become a riot of harsh tones. This is all a painter's palette because he or she knows instinctively that this is the way Spirit shows itself when you become clairvoyant. You are not far from that, my dear, and painting would be very therapeutic for you for as you close your eyes you would literally see those tones, those lights, those hues, the embodiment of what Spirit is and wants to represent. There is a closeness that we are sharing right now – I am sure you are feeling it: an awareness, a blending, a modulation, something new that was not there before – not just a voice – but literally a presence, an excitement for what the future is about to unfold and an acquaintance. We are becoming acquainted once again with one another, with one another's energy, with one another's way of saying something or of reacting or enacting. It can be bliss, my dear, and it shall be as this becomes a daily occurrence. We are there for one another in the joy, in the compatibility and the love that we speak of and that we show and feel and enact for one another. I am blessed my dear – not just you – for in your humility I know you would say: "How could such a gift happen? How could a treasure such as Quan Yin who is a Goddess for half of the planet happen? How is it we could interact as we do? How may I bring the message through faithfully?".

There is no secret, my dear – be only who you are; welcoming, loving, open to whatever it is that will unfold and that may occur because of you, because of the presence of this beautiful essence that we represent. You do not seem to marvel anymore that the miracle of opening vortices is yours, for it is a miracle, my dear, yet, because it is seeming more

3

familiar to you, you consider it a daily happening, something you could easily walk into, tune in to, feel the energy and know that there is something that is very monumental, but you are not surprised by it anymore. And, may I say, this is my point. We need not be surprised by one another's presence, for I love it when you are bowing before me with humility, with respect, with the giving of yourself and that which you dispose of to me, to the God source, and I, in turn, marvel that I am given the permission to be so close and intimate with you, that we may truly express our thoughts jointly, our feelings, what our heart is dictating to those who will come.

Be not surprised, my dear, by your reactions. I know you are ashamed that you reacted perhaps too strongly in your recent business meeting, but it was because I was present with you making you aware that such things as we witnessed, which was certainly a withholding of thoughts, a manipulation, a connivance, a scheming that was not open to inspection, existed.

This is not an accustomed habit I have, but we are still growing aware of one another. It will happen more often that you will react and I wish you to understand that it is because we are both jointly reacting and feeling what it is that is surrounding us. As you voice your opinions you may appear belligerent in your thinking; it is appropriate action, for if it were not, I would not be there and as you feel me, and as you know that we are working together, let those reactions be spontaneous, let them flow. You need not apologise although it is unusual behaviour for you. It was timely, for things were not going well in this department and you have been wise to disconnect from it. Your bodies will be drastically changed; you will be more feminine Mary – I am not saying you will put on weight – but certainly your facial structure will be far fuller and more loving. You will not be plump – as you are concerned about that – but you will expand in so many ways: of grace and charm and love, your voice will become harmonious and soft, melodious, you will be able to sing again and you will feel a freedom that you have not felt since you were a small child, a young girl of seven who suddenly decided it was too dangerous to be who she really was and shut down.

This is the time of openings my dear. Yes, we are all opening to love, we are opening to the God Source. We are opening to the Ascended Masters, to those who love us dearly and who wish to be with us in this momentous time. Changes will be everywhere and the news will not be good. You would perhaps do well not to watch so much of CNN, for as you have perhaps noticed, there are usually only horror stories that are repeated. The Discovery Channel is always a pleasant source of tuning in to what the planet is doing that is positive. Otherwise, we ask you please to study your notes, to go over what it is that you would like to teach and bit by bit you will be hearing messages of: "This would be good", or "That would be excellent". You may sing and you may be joyful and rejoice. Maybe a set of drums might be nice to pound upon or a harmonica and certainly the piano will be used by many of your students. I say "your students" for you do not believe it yet I know, but there are some, and quite a few, who will return often and finally they will be setting aside time in the future so that they will be sure to find a slot in your busy programming and wherever you go, there will be many. Many are lined up even outside your centres to ask if there is not someone who perhaps did not show up and they could take their place, or could you have an open forum for those who are so eager. Please, my dear, before you give in to this kind of request, we ask you to consult with us. I will be there with you and you will feel the answer. You can always ask me as you do at present whether this is correct or right for the highest good of all concerned and is it within God's purpose for the centre and for you as teachers. We must be aware that you are not to become too tired and, perhaps, living very close at hand might be a drain on your energies. If it is the case, then you will post someone to be in charge of watching the guest centre while the evening hours are transpiring. Someone might have a crisis in the midst of the night, but if you could alternate and perhaps two of you go to rest thoroughly, you might find it more peaceful. You will know as time goes by how much of your energy is drained and it will change from class to class. Maybe with others you will feel exuberant, you will feel filled with joy and the love of what you are doing along with new ideas, new ventures that will come to you that you have never done before. You might even take them out to the greenhouse and plant plants and seeds so that they can watch them grow and when they come back the next time they would see them in full bloom.

The weather will be far different, more clement. There will be winds but they will be less frequent. There will be a softness about the land, about the trees, about nature in general. You may all go and connect with the fairies. You may take bicycle rides. We will protect you and surround you with the light – an invisible screening that no one will know but all will feel safe and so happy. When you come back for hot chocolate or coffee or tea, or whatever it is that warms the soul, we will be with you as you sit around the fire and have an evening chat. It will be wonderful and people will be warming their toes, some will even be holding feet that have been frozen and they will warm them and love them and others will be cuddled up together, feeling the softness and the awareness that it's all right to touch, it's all right to connect, to be one group and to let their hearts speak and their voices tremble and the tears fall while saying they are not sure. They will dare to say what they are feeling and you will just listen with compassion, with open hearts and "it will happen". The miracles that you have wished for will suddenly happen and they will seem like: "Oh, that was so easy, I had no idea that if I spoke about it, it would lose all of its grip upon me, it would not be holding me in bondage and now that I can talk about it, it feels so simple, so easy and I can share". This will be freeing many from illnesses that have already begun. So, though you may not always see a radical healing – know that it is taking place. And, as I speak you wonder that all this is seeming so easy, yet you are thinking there must be something you need to do to make it happen. As you have found in your business meetings, you just need to show up. Once you are present, the ideas will come to you, the answers will be there. If you are meant to channel you will know it. If you are meant to just listen, perhaps to hold a hand or to caress a tearful face, you will also know it. Be not alarmed about what you haven't prepared or what you still need to study or, goodness knows, "What have I forgotten that we were supposed to do today?" Then they will look at you and you will burst out into laughter and say: "Well, what about having fun? What would be fun for everyone?", and they will say: "Well, this is certainly not a serious school and we are asked to pay for this?" But as they deal with one another and walk out of the door and skip and find their hearts are light, they discover something very wonderful that they hadn't known was there. It's a sort of treasure hunt and they will love it and they will be filled with their own success and the excitement of what happened.

There are so many things, my dear. We have not even begun to scratch the surface. All these souls may hug the crystals and ask for support – not just for themselves – but for their loved ones. We will be together and we will laugh and marvel and enjoy the fun for I truly rejoice in the thought of what is going to happen. It is a blessed occasion and I thank you for this partnership. I will be there when you need me and when I am there, welcome me and ask what it is that you can do to support this coming together. I leave you now in peace and love of the Holy Spirit, knowing you are protected. The light is always around you, my love, and you need not worry. However, if something is happening that you do not understand, call my name and I will be there immediately. You and I are bonded until the Earth shall need us no longer. I leave you and bless you and thank you. Goodbye, my dear.'

INTEGRITY IN THE SACRED ISLES

Kuthumi

'We, in the name of Spirit, say there must be integrity, there must be absolute honesty in what you are doing and undertaking. Although I sound like I am shouting, this is because we, on our side, are not going to support anything that has to do with devious behaviour or manipulation in the name of the dark forces, so, if I am standing here today you could visualise me standing on a rock with a whip and a torch in my hands. That torch is to light the way and the whip is to say to those who are not welcome: "Stand back in the name of Kali and fear that which is going to be your option, that which you have chosen, the way that you will be punished". In our anger to put down those forces, we will not tolerate anything that comes from the dark forces to be part of you and I say that for all of you, for there is such creativity here, there is such integrity and there is such a moving force that is behind you that as you come together, I believe you are beginning to feel this energy.

You went over that vortex this afternoon and asked what is a vortex. It could have come up out of the water it was so powerful, wanting to tell you this is what it is; it stands for the new generation. It stands for the new planet Earth, it stands for a new paradigm that is about to be executed here, on this very island, and you wonder why this place? Why does it have to be so special; there are other places doing the same kind of work?

8

And we say to you it has been a bastion of light, of energy. We, the protectors, part of the astral command and those who are members of the Spiritual Hierarchy, have chosen this spot as the source of divine energy. Do you see, it has to be the cradle where all of this shall start and manifest. When it is pure, it is going off to the fictional British Isle to become famous, to become open, to allow that exchange which is going on between the good and those who are trying to find the good and those who have not seen it there in their own hearts. So, I ask you please, do ask questions, come to me with whatever you are wanting to ask for I will in my capacity of power answer you as Kali knows what kind of power has been needed to protect this island from the dark forces. We have put an invisible bubble around this island so that nothing can penetrate here that would violate the kind of integrity that we are looking for and that we are creating amongst you and with you. We are stimulating you when you are asleep, bringing you in new energy that you have not had before, nor would have anywhere else. This is why we want this space to be sacred.

We want you to come here to know what it is, what it will be, how you are going to create it, what are the principles that you must stand by, what it is that is going to be done here on this very planet and how it shall start in these sacred islands. So, if you will proceed with your questions, I would be happy to hear from you.'

'We look to Mary for support. How can she most consciously use those resources which have been entrusted to her care?'

'A very appropriate question, for many say she is stupid, she is lazy, she is doing things that are not acceptable anywhere, but she has listened and her guidance has been one with Spirit. She has been told that it shall be provided as a forum for many to come. We are speaking of the humble, we are speaking of those not necessarily in terms of financial basis, but those who will come with their hearts open, who are asking Spirit:

9

"Please give me that opportunity that I have not had through the system". What the system does provide is: it will give benefits on the one hand, and then it will sweep away any gains in the form of taxes and punishments to people who have not had the wherewithal to withstand this onslaught of greed. So, this is a place where it shall be gentle, where people will come and open their hearts. They will be allowed to cry and they will say: "I have not been supported, I have not felt this love before". This is where we are going to watch these little children; we are going to watch the angels coming out of the land to support these children. We want you to stand up for it, as well. Mary has chosen this as her path, to help those who are not helpless but who have not seen the Light, who do not understand what Spirit represents. You shall be the living incarnation – all of you – of that which Spirit has told you to bring in, in this lifetime.

I am not telling you things that you have not heard before – you have chosen this before you were incarnated. Your paths have crossed now for a reason. As you come together, you are discovering one another and saying: "You can do this, you can do that and look at how it could come together, and create something that would bubble like a fountain". Everyone will see it and they will marvel. They will not dare to touch you because I, Kali, will not allow it. I will protect you and will stand there but I cannot protect something that has not been tested by Spirit and has not stood up for the truth. Here I ask once again that you check in with your Guides. It can be those who bring in other entities as well but you must always ask who are you representing. Are you speaking the truth for your level, which is one of an earthly third dimension? If so, you cannot know the truth; it is not there where you will find it nor in a library nor in an encyclopaedia nor in a Law School. The truth is not spoken on this Earth. It is certainly not the kind of thing that is paying its way.

In order to find the truth, you need to go into a monastery, a sacred place and bow down and become as humble as the worms and the insects that crawl on the ground. That is your path; to show others that you have your skills, you bring them

10

together to develop something that will be warm and open and will allow the flow for all kinds of energies from many dimensions. Some will be visible, some will not be visible but the energy shall be felt. It will be like a current going around you – much as this water as you look out. You will see the current that is pushing the water around you and that will be protecting you, allowing those to come to you who are meant to come and those who are not meant to come will not withstand that wall of energy. They will say: "We do not know why, but we don't like it here; it's uncomfortable; we're not part of this group; we don't want to come" and that is what you will come to acknowledge and realise that you may ask for what you want to come and who you would like to have as your students and who will send out the messages to the world.'

'Mary asked where we will be going in the next five to ten years. What are the kind of things that we are going to be focusing on? What will be our role and responsibility as time goes on? Where shall we be focusing our efforts for the future?'

'I would say that it is time that you get your names out there. Create the name whatever it is, create a logo and go boldly on. Start producing videos, start publishing books, use comic strips – whatever it is that you need to do. Within five years from now people will say this is the Walt Disney of the next era and they will look to you for inspiration. So, once again, as you are looking for the genius in the Law division or genius in the World Bank or whatever your expertise is, look for those who are creative and can enhance that which you will do so splendidly.

Can you imagine a film about your work? It would be very successful I tell you, and it is not a time to be modest. It has been your way and I honour you for this. It has been outstanding. It is time now to say this is the kind of thing that we want to give to the world: show it in Russia, show it in China – you don't need words, you can put subtitles under the page, but

11

you can get it out and say we are caring about you, but this caution I say to you; it must be caring and it must not come across that we are exploiting the public and they are credulous and adhering to what we are saying as if it was a gospel – it must be pure, there must be absolute censorship. There is a committee out there that is reviewing anything that is going out for publication and how it is being used, for some might take the film, cut it up and put in another bit and say it is your film. Again, you must look at your rights of publishing and any kind of necessary steps that need to be taken to protect patents. So, it will be powerful and no matter where you go there will be a banner that is raised and people will come to cheer you and want to hear from you, even to touch your garments – such will be the way, for they shall be terrified by this new time that is coming when we will go into darkness, when the planet seems to be spinning into another orbit and there is daylight full time every day. What is going on? What are we to do?

They will bow down, they will be on bended knees, they will look to some source for inspiration, for support, for guidance, and we want it to be you, we have decreed this. Can you see the power that is behind you and acknowledge that it is going to propel you as fast as any of those speedy motor boats, as fast as any vehicle can go on this Earth? You shall move forward rapidly which means you have to have everything in order before you can declare yourself to the world. Is that clear?'

'What does the vortex look like that will define our group?'

'It is not yet formed and I would prefer to wait on that when you are together as a group. The group is not totally gathered yet and there are members who are not here, so I would prefer it when all the energy is gathered and then we shall allow it to come through the centre of your group.'

'How can this effort best serve as a Guide for others who are trying to make their capital work more consciously? What are the most beneficial endeavours that could be engaged in, in the next two or three years?'

'First of all, it is integrity and corporate firms know that their firms, in order to operate well and efficiently, must be based on integrity. Every department is to analyse how much integrity there is; why are they doing it; what are they motivated by. Do you see, the famous dollar cannot be the measuring stick – I believe you say "the benchmark" – any longer. What is coming out is how much are they willing to give part of their knowledge away; they must subsist, they must make money, they must succeed, but inasmuch as they are out there giving and bringing in new knowledge, converting it into something new that is needed and giving that away, bringing it in again – this is the way life works. How do you think we work on those other dimensions? We do not hold knowledge, we are there to give it to you, to give it to others who are coming to us asking for help. Your planet is bubbling with ideas, with evolution, with Spirit and you are there to capture it and they will say: "How did you do it?". Well, you are not holding it; if you squeeze it too hard – imagine an ice-cream cone: you've crushed it and it's dribbling and it's all over you and that's what is going to happen to those who are greedy. They must know there is a law that will not stand for any kind of devilishness or manipulation or greed or pulling in towards the centre. A strong central focus in an organisation that holds together whereby people trust one another, but by giving and coming and giving and pulling back in again, to analyse it in ten years' time, that will be the magic. You will have tasted it before but it will not be existing always in your centres, but as time goes by the magic will be there and people will be taught how to work with magic, how to respect magic, how to create magic, for magic is nothing more than working with the elementals, working with the little folk and the fairies and the trees.

Life itself is full of magic and you have seen it when you have gone to some of these beautiful places, admired them and looked at a sunset and gasped: "Where did that sunset come from? Where is it that these rainbows have their source? How is it that they occur when we need encouragement? What is happening that is sponsoring us?" Things like the Northern Lights will start happening again and you will say: "But this is not for us, this is for the whole world to see". Yes, but it is for you, it will be your show and you will say to people: "Come and you will observe magic – we don't know what kind – but it will happen". Whole cathedrals will appear before you, my dears, can you imagine? Suddenly, a lawn is transformed into a beautiful cathedral. If you go to Glastonbury in England and you see the remains of what is left of that beautiful cathedral, it is in the grass, there are just walls but could you imagine a complete and magnificent structure?

There will be shrines, there will be Tibetan types of worship centres. There will be all kinds of beings who will come and will find their shrine on these centres – bow down before it. You might not even know what it represents. What is a stupa? What does it look like? You might say you don't know, but you haven't called upon it. You have just said to people come and receive, open your heart for the heart is the key. And, as they open their hearts and you feel the tears are coming in their eyes, welcome them with love. The more you open your love and they receive it, the more that interaction will create within itself a vortex and that vortex will allow you to see into the future. It will allow you to behold that there are beings below the Earth and there are connections above you and all dimensions might come at once, or it might be just a parade of one and then another and you say: "But look, look at what's going on", and people will marvel, they will know that when they come to your spaces, magic will exist and it will not die out. If you are in integrity and you see to it that all of your companies are directed from that centre of integrity, then there is no foolishness: you have checks and balances, you maintain that criteria, there can be no abuse because we shall be with you. If something comes up, we will inform you and you shall know about it in time. This was our gift to inform Mary that this abuse is going on.

So, do not be fearful of any consequences that might come

14

about as a result of your boldness. They know they have done wrong and the firmer you stand and the more that you are able to say your truth and your convictions, any abuser will cower for they cannot sustain the energy that is coming from all of you. Are there other questions?'

'What does Mary need to make her heart sing?'

'She needs to get out in nature, and I do thank you for that question. She knows it, yet comes back confused and tired and will go to bed. If she could walk around the island at least three times before going to bed, that would be the remedy; even walk elsewhere, but at the moment it is not safe for her to walk along a beach or walk out of the property at night or in early dawn. It would be preferable that she walk around here, go through the garden and marvel at what is going on. She can start her Maggie Magpie productions right here on this island, talking to the trees, talking to the plants, the fairies – whatever she conceives; a star – whatever she would choose to do. She must take note as she is outside during her promenade around the island. That will be the beginning of her creative work, for her creative work is almost as a child would be seen in an invisible form above a mother who is about to expect a child; that child is there and waiting to be integrated and as for her, her creativity is out there, is waiting for her to realise that she has this potential and all it means is enacting it and bringing it forth and having a pen and paper everywhere she goes so that she may write her notes. She needs to start creating and not holding in the darkness and the deception and the betrayal – those are not good emotions for her right now, she does not need them. So, if you could stress to her the need right now to get out and interact with nature and friends who like nature, it would be appropriate.

So, if there is nothing more to ask right now, I believe your friend will bring in a very beautiful energy to close this session and I will leave you for the moment but, I beg of you, come back to me as I am there to heal with Mary, I am there to see to it that her work is carried out and make sure that this is a safe terrain to allow Quan Yin to interact with all of you. As you know, she is the gentlest and wisest of Bodhisattvas that this Earth has ever seen and I provide the security for her. So, I will leave you now and bless you and say to you I thank you for listening. I feel very happy right now that you have asked for my presence though you did not know who was coming. I shall be back to guide you if you do need me and I, Kali, say to you blessings from the Holy Spirit and shall all this be in the hands of the Almighty and that there shall be no error here as to who is whom and who worships and bows down before the divine.'

* * *

'Welcome. Thank you.'

'It's so wonderful to see such wonderful children gathered around and yet who come here from so many directions. All are united together with faith and love and this wonderful process will grow greater and stronger. Welcome, dear ones. I am St Francis. I come here quite often, but to feel the energy that is here and around here is wonderful. Yes, dear Mary?'

'Kuthumi, could you tell me something about Kali? It's quite an extraordinary energy, I'm not quite used to it and wonder that sometimes it sounds angry?'

'No dear one. It's almost like the judge of the judges, even though there are none. She becomes as one and as strong as she is to send a message clearly to the universe so well spoken and clear she is actually doing that through you and through others and it is wonderful to have her almost energising you.'

'Are you saying this is Quan Yin? Quan Yin and Kali are the same?'

'Indeed. They united many, many years ago and it's the connection that you have together with them.'

16

'So, indeed, Kali will protect me?'

'At all times. If you ask, you will be protected.'

'Is there anything in particular I might need to be protected from?'

'The wisdom that I can give you is don't put everything into one basket, but, at the same time, don't remove them all from there, take part of it from there and put it where you know you can make profit over night, every second as we are talking right now. I suggest you clean up the house completely. In other words, trim those dead branches and let only those that are willing to grow healthy be part of it.'

'If you read books about your life there is a dispute whether the Pope was supportive of you or a kind of thorn in your side as you were trying to do your work. Which way was it?'

'It's a sad story dear one. It is not one I wish to have published.'

EXPERIENCING THE OUTER REALMS

Shendoah

'I come from the sphere that is far above, that seems so far away yet hearts bring me close to you all. My name is Shendoah and I come to you from the family of Sananda. Mary knows me well – I was her beloved son and this is my first time ever connecting through her in a voice. So, if you will forgive me, we shall be very gentle this morning and we will bring our hearts in alignment, together so that this duality, this "couple" if you will, to express our oneness as coming together, and as we come together I will spread myself out in my energy and I will enclose you all within my arms as those who are the family of my mother are also my family. You may say to me: "But what is it that gives you authority to speak to all of us?", and I will say it has been many years now since I have been in the higher realms, have experimented with this universe, with the universe that is beyond. I have been with most of the Ascended Masters that you know of: Sananda, Kuthumi, Master Hilarian, Metitron, Melchisedeck – who has also been my Guide and mentor. I have been given the opportunity to experiment with other planets, with beings that are not humanoids, that have no idea of the concepts that you are dealing with. I have been through and experienced most of what you would experience as a dying process: coming into embodiment in another realm, in another cellular body, interacting with others and finding it so different and freeing.

Nothing is holding you, nothing is compulsive or impulsive; you flow with that love, you flow with the light, you flow with the angelic sphere and those Guides who come to you and tell you now it is time for you to learn this lesson. We bid you well and here is your exercise and off you go and do the best you can and come back to your Guides and say: "I have done that, I do hope you approve – now where do I go?". So, do you see, I am saying this so you will understand that we, too, on our level do not know what the future holds – whether this is our next lesson or is it the place we are to stay for some extended period? We are always asking, we are always reaching out to those who are coming to us in that angelic light and in an embodiment that we can sometimes see, sometimes hear, sometimes only feel. We are open more to our sensitivity than you are but we are still experiencing events, people, tasks – much as you are – as a learning experience. And, as we come back from each experience, we cannot say we know it all, we can only say we have felt this, we have been with that and we know this kind of person would be longing for that kind of treatment. So it is as a learner that I come to you, for my lessons have been well learned they tell me on this higher level and now I wish to interact with Earth which my mother and I did when I was still in her realm. I come to you with open arms and with an open heart. I may say that there are other Guides here that are present so that we are not alone. They are bringing and accentuating the energy around us; they are present for each one of you.

Can you imagine having a Guide behind each chair? You might want to communicate with them in which event I will let them speak through this vehicle, but, first of all, may I answer your questions as I do see you have come together with many and ask what it is you would like to say to me?'

'Last night we were outside and I think we met you. Were you there on the fence or were you behind us?'

'I was behind you and I thank you for recognising me for there was much activity and there was much that would

19

distract you from what you were looking at as other lights would appear, but you did not lose your focus and when you chose to look at an object or a blinking light, you stayed with it. We all marvelled at you and at your abilities and at the love that you extended outward in that small area; although it seemed small, it was magnified on the higher levels and was quite brilliant. So, you had your own show and we are having another right now as the rain is coming to calm and soothe all that has been parched and dried by the sun. It is only another phase of what you are to experience and we on our level are enjoying it for rain is not a part of our life on that higher realm. It is not higher my dears, we are not above you, we are in you and around you, we are just not visible. Even as you become an Ascended Master and you rise and think you will see it all, there may be a presence that has no light and does not do more than pass through you, and you say: "Where did it come from and where is it going and what is the message it left?". But it only came to greet you and to walk through you. So, there is magic on all levels and you need to open yourself to it and do not judge it. Do not want to know all about it – just feel it, experience it, laugh with it, enjoy it, and that is all it is meant to be.'

'Are you able to tell me where this magic will take me?'

'I thank you for that question, that is brilliant, my dear one and we are marvelling at your change and the metamorphosis that is going on within you and around you and you are far more receptive than you have ever been and now you are coming into your own. As you feel things, express them, let them out – for they need to flow through you – try not to hold on to them. They are as a little child: you may rock it and love it but you put it back in its place to let it sleep and renew itself. So, as you ask these questions, may I say to you what we are trying to explain is that you will soon be us, you will be so open and sensitive to these beings that are around you that you will just take on what they are telling you. They might even be standing within you when you are moving your hands and are demonstrating something. Whatever you are doing is what they are doing in you: they are speaking through you because they love you for no other reason than the fact they are here because they love you. They love this planet and they love all beings and want them to come to you as they will come to them. So, do you see, there is not theirs and ours, there is not us and you; there is a melding going on within this group this very moment and it is bringing all of you to understand and to share and to marvel at one another for you shall do that. As you see someone brilliant lighting up a space which is enormous and you say: "But how did that person do that; I thought I knew her or I knew him and look at the way people are reacting to that being". It is all of us coming together to funnel that particular message, that guidance, that beingness and that light that you are carrying which is already in place. So, you have merely to open the door; it may be open at this moment; you want to open it a little further and look out before you go fully and you like what you see then open it further and you might open it this way as well and say: "Yes, I feel comfortable with my new friends; I will be that which they are wanting me to be", and you will be so open and beautiful and loving, enhancing, enchanting, that people will come and see things you had no idea were there. You did not know you stood for something. You did not know you represented beauty or light or poetry or the gift of simply touching someone – you might reach out and touch them and they will be changed forever. The yogis do that and you shall do it for all of you shall gain those abilities together and there must be togetherness and bonding within this group, for if one person ascends and the others are left behind, you will be devastated. All of you are learning from each other in probably the fastest growth you have experienced in a very long time. So let me not go on forever. Are there other questions?'

'Please, I ask why do I feel an attraction to a higher realm?'

'There is a part of you, my dear, that has connected with a heavenly sphere and that is the longing you have desired for so

21

very long. It is there, becoming more predominant within your heart and it is as if your humanness can no longer be comfortable with that longing until it has been satisfied. It is opening you as you have never been opened, my dear. Experience it; let that sadness happen, for you were so close once upon a time and you did not ascend, you came back with great sadness.

So, you are experiencing it again, not knowing if you may be joyful or disappointed. It is your time to be joyful, my dear. You have given so much to this planet, to your family, to your extended family for distances that are immeasurable and now you must know that you can trust, trust that you can open your longing to all that you have wanted and all that you are allowed to experience – no one, nothing is holding you back any longer. It is your choice and your soul will be happy to explain to you what is happening in more detail if you would like further instructions, but you are expanding at such a rate and at such a phenomenon that you are worried that you will get up there again and say: "Yes, I am ready and they will tell you no". That will not happen again, just enjoy it, be on all levels – whatever you choose to be is there where you are supposed to be. If you would speak to St Germain he would be very happy to be with you and realign you if that's what you are asking for or to bring you simply answers. Are there other questions?'

'How is Mary to deal with confrontation?'

'Very good that question, for she cannot grow until she overcomes her fear and part of her fear was being dealt with this morning in confrontation. It was not coming out as something that was angry or belligerent or trying to teach a lesson to somebody to put them down. It came in a space of openness and clearing and being light and free enough to say what is in your heart – that is not confrontation and as she has experienced this and known that it is okay, it is safe then she can go forward and say: "I can deal with anyone, for if I come from a space of love, there is no confrontation". It is only done as a clearing as you would do when you heal somebody – you push it away and you let it go and that is what is to be

22

happening here as you open yourselves up and you clear up and you let it go, it's gone. If more comes up, then you are ready to deal with it but it is not confrontational, it does not mean because you speak your truth that you will lose your job or be demoted or be an outcast and no one will ever speak to you – it is comforting, it is like you are holding hands right now and saying thank you for sharing, thank you for being strong and open and trusting that it is all right to speak your truth. Do you see, even the Gods are forgiving you and supporting you in your truth.'

'Dear, ask your Guides, what you need to do at this time.'

'May I say to you, one and all, that each class that comes in will be different. There may be classes where you are required to teach each and every one of you, there may be classes where you merely share. You might be opening your sensitivities to one another, learning the lesson of interacting with energies. You might be bringing in entities that have been present around you and that will choose to give a lesson that particular day. It will vary and your astuteness will be measured as you do write up a curriculum, for you will have to deal with all of this and put it in such terminology that it will not look New Age or undecided or that this is a group who really do not have anything to teach but are putting in a lot of flowery words to make it sound good. It must have substance and yet they must know that it may vary according to the dynamics of the group, that there is no accident, that whatever happens is because it is meant to happen and to put that into words will be a challenge for each and every one of you. So no one has the key as of now.'

'Where are we to find ideas and inspiration?'

'You will receive it, perhaps when you are together, perhaps when you are meditating. You may be separate and walking through the woods or climbing a tree and you get a message and that is the message that you are to write down immediately

23

and bring back to the group and, may I say here and now, the group will be an extended group and decision making will take place on an extended level. The core group to which you refer will see to it that everything is handled in proper order, that finances are taken care of, communications are taken care of – each one will have his and her aspects but as to the teachings, they are not going to be a decision by this core group. If they like the teachers, yes of course they may have something to say but as to what is going to be taught and how, the core group must have openness and freedom to the extent that people may flow with their intuition as you will, all of you, for you will constantly be given new information, it will never be the same. One group may have been a tremendous success but if you try to apply those same principles to the next group it will fail and there you will be severely challenged. So, as you are opening yourselves and experiencing Spirit and meditating together and finding the bonding and the love, the miracles will happen.'

'Will we have prescribed times to "experience one another's teachings"?'

'Indeed and you will interact together as you will have a set time to come together and share what is going on, but one must not make the decisions for the other; the competencies are different, the requirements are different but there must be spontaneity within this group, there must be enlightenment, there must be creativity in all dimensions. Someone might be teaching metaphysics and suddenly say: "I want to teach pottery, I think people need something tangible to get their hands into and if they are angry, let them punch it out in a bunch of clay". You see, it's got to flow and inasmuch as you feel it flowing and you feel it congruous and harmonious, then it is working and you do not know how it is working nor do you need to know how – that is our work. As you are working, we are working and there are other dimensions above us that are working. We all want to see this happen and that no one has an exclusivity, no one has a pattern to say this is only my stuff, you cannot have it, for as you give it and you are letting it flow freely through you, then more will come in, more magic, more experiences, more demands. Your time will be so precious that you can only give maybe half an hour to one or to a group and you have to fly off to New Zealand or you might be asked to go to Hawaii; there is a group awaiting you and they do not even know you are coming, so you must rush to get to them. Do you see, it is all interacting – Spirit, humanness, extraterrestrials, guidance, centeredness, for that polarity is extremely valid and valuable and if there is not an attachment to a polarity on your level then you will be thrown out of orbit and you might lose yourselves and say: "Well I'm not good in this group. I will go to another group" and orbit around that. There is to be something similar to a gravitational force that will bring you all back to centre. Do you see, you come into that wonderful bonding that you had over the vortex and that feeling of oneness – you are one with each other, you are one with the land, you are one with all of the beings that were above you and around you. There was only one, there is only oneness in being with God and as you experience that and as that Love and Light flow through you, then we shall interact with you more and better and faster and you might have a message for one person that is just the key to what they wanted and they will say: "Thank you very much, I got what I came for", and they will leave.'

'You must remain open and sensitive to what is happening in the moment?'

'At first, you need to test your mettle, you need to know how you interact – what are the dynamics, to feel one another, to see how one group works perhaps before another and another group comes in. If you have a full house, you have thirty people and each person is demanding and requiring attention, you shall be very busy. And you, who promote your healings, massage – they will love it to the point that everyone will want two a day and then three a day – you cannot be everywhere. You will need to be out there supporting one another. Maybe you decide this is a Sunday so one team will come in and then Monday that team has relaxation and the other team comes in. Do you see, the teaching group will have to be expanded and expanding and as you work well together in this one centre then you will take your techniques and move them elsewhere and try your skills so that the ultimate goal is that you will be working in all of these centres simultaneously, but you must proceed slowly, it cannot happen in one go otherwise one centre would say: "We know what we are doing and we want to stay here, but we do that speciality", and another centre will say: "Well we know our field as well, we're doing our speciality". What we want you to know is that you are working with us and that we will choose what is to come through and will work with each of you, so there is no one speciality in one area nor another speciality in another area. You will be known as the magical group.

As you come in, maybe two come in, and you represent the group. But the group will grow and expand and there will be more and more and then you will see at that later time how it works for you. All decisions cannot be made right here and now and it must include all of you. So if you could all be present; we could sit down with you as a group, have you mediate and bring in more knowledge. Knowledge is not an exclusivity and what you are being given right now is new knowledge. You have all been given openings to things that you had no idea that you knew and maybe they will come out within the group, maybe they will come out three weeks later when there is a class and you say: "My, I had no idea – what is it that I am talking about? Is this wrong, is this off balance?" and others will come back to you with incredible feedback. So, do not limit yourselves, that is all I am saying. You must feel comfortable at all moments, to share. If you could have a time in the morning to come together much as a football huddle would be: you group around each other and hold each other and give each other courage and then after the day is over, sit down and be together again, to feel was it all right; is this what I am comfortable with, is somebody not comfortable because he or she had too much work? That is also an important part of the bonding and working well together, to support one another. Change is the essence and it shall be change and do not fear it for change is always beneficial. Are there more questions?'

'I would like to ask if my Guide who is with me today has any message for me?'

'It is Archangel Michael, my dear, and he would like you to know to dwell in peace for you need not take on the worries of those that you care about so dearly. If you could trust, ask Spirit once, twice are they all right, is my daughter all right, is my son doing well, is this one all right and as you get a yes or a no, then release it. If it is a no, then you may want to call them or to enquire further, but if you get a yes, release it, my dear. You love them so dearly that you hold them still in your energy field and you must learn to let them go, for in releasing them, you will benefit tremendously and they will feel it, as well. "Mother trusts us and she loves us and knows that we will do the right thing", they will say. Archangel Michael is with you and around you and he will come to you, my dear.'

'I have a question concerning the order of how you want to open the world up to the learning centres, as you call them, as Mary calls them rather, and I wonder if the Isle would be first. Do you have any idea about the others or any sort of semblance of which direction they may unfold or which may be first?'

'We, as a part of the Spiritual Hierarchy, have deemed the Isle the most likely the best place to start because of the energy that is coming in from that part of the globe. It is much like this energy in the sense that it is virgin: it has not been overdeveloped or tainted by any kind of doctrine except the dread and the threat of the IRA. As that settles down, people are more willing to open up and to look at new ways of dealing with their lives, new ways of dealing with emotions, relationships, happiness and the lack of. We feel that you would have much success. What most likely will happen is people will come to you and say: "Would you come and speak at my church? Would you come and be a part of my meditation group? Would you tell us some of the things that you are telling us here?" In which event, you will have to make that decision. Are you able to travel? Would one person be enough to go and speak to a large group on behalf of the group? These are new concepts for you and not all can afford to come to the centre though they may come for only four days, but it is the travel in itself and that needs to be their responsibility. So, by moving a nucleus of your core group or whatever you choose to call it, of your teaching staff, of whomever you choose to go, then you could spread yourselves more quickly – do you see? So, this again is validating the fact that you will need to be numerous. You must not be stepping on each other's feet. So, indeed, as you train one group you will come into another area to train another group taking into consideration what the climate is, what are the politics? Is this a good time to start or is it still threatening?'

'How is this energy affecting me?'

'I would like to include all of you, my dears, who are present. I would like no one excluded. There is an energy present here. Something has happened within all of your energy fields. Imagine bubbles coming together. Do they burst or do they meld one in another when they take on new hues, new colouring? All of you have been stimulated by the presence of others. Some you would say may not be always affected positively but what is making you look at your own issues is always positive. So, as the group has been willing to share and open up, your energy field as a group is expanding and this is something valuable to teach the world when they say: "But my worst enemy is preventing me from doing what I want to do most". You can testify here, in this group; enemies are very valuable and very helpful in that they make you look at what it is that you are not doing well, why do you offend, what is the problem, what is it I am looked upon as and why do I trigger buttons? So, it is all positive.

28

We on our level like the dynamics that are happening within this group. We cherish all of you as individuals. We want to see this harmony happening and as this harmony occurs there will be a miracle and more miracles can happen in small pods when you will have a group come together who really don't get on, and, as you work through them and with them as separate groups, then you begin to see the whole group coming together and when that happens, they will not want to leave. They will say: "But we cannot leave this place, we cannot leave you; as people we love you, we cherish the connections we have made and not realising where they have come from and how far they have gone, but they will never forget the work that is being done in these centres – we can guarantee that."'

'Will there be a fifth centre?'

'My dear, there will not just be a fifth, there will be eleven of them and you must be prepared to open yourselves. Someone, no doubt, will come in and say: "I can sponsor a centre; you do not have to build it for me but I need your energy, I need your input, I need your presence". And some of the healers might want to be a part of that centre as it grows. So, do you see, some will come in to learn your skills and they will go out; others will come in to learn.

So you will constantly be creating, reproducing, magnifying, distributing and then you will say: "Look, look what has happened – Malta is a centre, Nassau is a centre, Bolivia is a centre, South Africa is a centre and then suddenly China might be interested – can you imagine opening up China?" And you will speak Chinese and say: "How is this? I don't speak Chinese but they understand me; I'm not sure what I am saying but they understand and they want a centre here. Can you see the excitement that will grow and it needs to be excitement, it needs to move, it needs to be dynamic, it needs to be challenged my dears for that is growth."'

'Can you tell me more about Kuthumi?'

'Kuthumi is behind you my dear and Kuthumi is a very healing energy and has been through much of this and you would perhaps do well to tune into Kuthumi. At this moment he is very interested in vortexes and certainly this porthole has been part of his doing. As you deal with him, you will understand where you and he relate. Where is the parallel? What is it that he has done and experienced that you are going to experience or have experienced? He can be extremely helpful to you, my dear for he has also known mutilation and harm and death and rising again from that phoenix to becoming who he was and who he is now, and so beautiful and so cherished by the entire globe. I honour you, my dear, for you have had perhaps the greatest struggle of all present and it has been a very, very sad experience for you to be one of the most beautiful people upon this earth and to find your body is not the same. It is going to change for you my dear as you trust and as you open your heart and know that within five months' time you shall be very different and you shall know how it has happened and why it has happened and in that way you can guide others. It is beautiful, you have accepted this and we honour you.

You will be extremely effective as a group and you will open yourselves in different directions in the way you feel that you would like to interact with the local population. There will be so much to share, so much to learn, so much to experience. It will be somewhat like this island of green, this magical land that has opened itself to you. It was not like that before – others may say it was – but it came alive as you arrived and now it is just saying it is time to be quiet today; you might want to rest, read a book or just enjoy each other by playing a game. We want it to be playful, my dears, and there is a lovely time when you can sit and be quiet when the storm is surging around you and telling you to go inwards. Is there more?'

'What is it I need to do?'

'Whatever is enjoyable, what is fun, what is playful, what is sheer delight for you – it might be eating an ice-cream cornet.'

'Is Master Hilarian near?'

'Yes my dear. It is Master Hilarian and he is wanting to heal you because he works with Master Metitron very closely and that is, as you know, on a higher dimension. The grid system is up there and when it is merely Master Hilarian who can recognise what it is you are needing then the grid will be adjusted. So would you speak to him and interact with him as a healer to another healer? He knows you well, my dear. You have studied together and worked on other universes together. There is much love and compassion and he does like a good laugh.

If that is all then I will leave you in peace and love and the fellowship of the Holy Spirit and wish you well, my dears, for there is so much that is coming to benefit you all as individuals and as a group and we are very proud of you. I say to you thank you for receiving me. I go in peace and leave you.'

DEALING WITH NEGATIVE ENERGY

Quan Yin

'I apologise for the hesitation. You were clearing out some of that negative energy that Mary just took on in your room and I do believe you need to deal with that.'

'What is going on in there?'

'It is an Indian force that has come in wanting to attack those that are up on the hill and, by attacking you, they feel that they are getting a kind of revenge for you have been carrying that Indian energy on this property for the white man and it is troublesome to see that they are playing with your energy though you do know you are protected and they could not reach you except to put you in a kind of semi-daze and not able to grapple with facts, so we let you sleep and rest and were working on you. They were only able to reach a part of you which seems to be paralysing only your ability to move your limbs and to react in your body but we were working on the essential part of you which they could not contact and because they could not reach it, they reinforce their power and have made it even more demanding and insistent to come towards you. So we wish you to go in and smudge yourself with sage. It would be appropriate if all three of you would walk together and you do not all need the smudge stick but you would carry the light and my energy into your room and set up a force-field with chosen crystals that you would like to have in your room and they will spend the rest of the time with you in your room, protecting you.'

'They seem to bring up a lot of dreams about conflict and "bad guys, good guys", that type of thing.'

'Part of you was reacting to their invasion of your base and of wanting to deal blows to you when you did not deserve it. We are very sorry, my dears, but we thought you would pick it up and you did very cleverly with your friends. Sometimes this is brought to your attention in ways that seem rather surprising, but the point needed to be driven home, so that you would understand that it is very necessary when you feel that energy to withdraw from it and stand back and ask Spirit: "What do I do about it now?". So you do not just accept it because it is in your space.'

'Did this come in last night?'

'It has been coming in at regular intervals but not so intensely as last night and today.'

'Was it here last year?'

'No it was not – this is a different energy. They are seeing your power and feel very threatened by it and they felt that because you had that alliance and almost that blood connection to the Indians that you would be the one they could control and you would speak for them and do their devilish work. They did not understand your true force and the protection you have, so they are rather puzzled right now as to why you are still functioning and you are feeling all right. So, before you do your healing this evening, it would be appropriate to cleanse it and put the crystals around and bring in as much white light as you can to bathe it and wash it and you might speak to the little crystal outside, your friend Arielle, and ask Arielle to protect that space and never let it be violated again.'

'Thank you. Could I use sage to smudge the room?'

'That would be very appropriate to burn up any residue of energy they have left behind.'

'Would this also be appropriate to protect a group from invasive entities?'

'That would be very, very good.'

'I find it interesting that my other friends who have a close connection to the Indians were not the target.'

'No my dear. That is an astute question but in this event it was the right spiritual energy that was coming in to heal. While you were seemingly paralysed and could not move, they took the advantage to cleanse and clear you. You may be noticing that there is a stepping up of the energy around you, to clear out that which you do not want in your bodily system as well as the energy around you, the people who surround you and who were pulling at your energy – that will improve tremendously now. In three weeks' time you will hardly remember what it was before and you will clear out all of that which is not needed cellularly in your body and we would recommend exercise – perhaps if you could do walking each day but do it with pleasure and take the time for you knowing that there is nothing more pressing than the time that is required for you and your body and your health. If you have access to some kind of machines – we might recommend a rowing machine to be very good to get those muscles moving around your upper torso because a lot of those fatty cells will start to be washed out of your system and as you reinforce those emotions, that will reinforce the muscle tone and give it more of a sleek look.'

'I was thinking that when I got to the Isle I was going to set myself with an exercise programme there.'

'And the Nordic Track or whatever it is you call it would

34

also be good for your legs and getting that motion but only if it is comfortable my dear – do not punish yourself.'

'I'm not going to punish myself. I've done it that way in the past.'

'Yes, and it would discourage you in the long run. Swimming as you know, is very beneficial and rids you of the toxins as you do this with pleasure. I believe you will find more delight in your own body as these three months take their time to heal and to beautify – if I may use that expression – to beautify you and your energy and it will not be long before you marvel at how beautiful you are and hold that energy as a treasure for it is something you have earned and worked for very hard and your beauty will only enhance the messages that you bring through. People will look to you with great admiration and want to be like you in many ways.'

'Thank you.'

'Have you other questions?'

'Not really specific questions. I think I'd just like to hear what you would like to say to me about the next six months coming up for me and the group.'

'Excellent. I would be very honoured to do so. You have new Guides coming in, my dear, and these are Guides that have been around you but always gave way to your principal Guides: Archangel Michael, Melchisedeck, Sananda – those you have treasured. There are many angels – Simeon is coming back to be with you and around you. You will also find other archangels, Gabriel for example shall be near you and you will also be aligned to a higher energy which is more of a universal energy. It has to do with that other universe where you have been and where you come and go from when you are not needed on this universal plane and that is an

35

energy – I would prefer not to say his name right now, it will come a time when he will want you to know his name and perhaps you might find it. He might give it to you in your meditations, but he is called the distant Spirit and he comes from very far away to be with you principally. You work well together when you are in that other universe and now it is a critical time for you because much of the evil is coming out of the Earth and it does not mean you will attract it but it will come and brush by you and want to cling to something they feel is solid, is pure, and if they could have a bit of you they would like to pull your energy and disperse it. This Guide is coming in as well as Simeon to dispel that and not allow them to touch you. So, you shall be very sacred and known in the universe of the angels and archangels as a very light, bright light. Imagine that column and have it shimmering in white light. That is what your energy will look like on those other fields and it is also welcoming to you to be in groups, for the more you gather groups around you and you talk to them, you will step into that next way of healing that you were asking about. Do not have too numerous groups. It would be best to contain the groups to, say, fifteen not more; with more you would not be able to relate to individuals but if there were as many as fifteen gathered in the Isle, you will feel the energy when it is bright and what group would like you to be in what space. Know that you will be familiar with working with their characteristics and where they need help and what kind of help. When you see one who is greedy, for example, but does not know it, and tends to collect things and hold them and not let them flow out and be generous of Spirit, you will be able to tune into that person immediately and tell them of their blockages. If they are offended and leave then that is a blessing; you do not need that energy around you. So, do not be afraid of your truth, it is as Archangel Michael's sword – it has that power, it may cut through something that would be very troublesome to you or to others and has been in the past. So, if you wish to visualise his sword, it is not a blue sword, it is a silver one with a golden handle and is slightly curved. As you bring that in, you might wield it about the room to cleanse the energy before they come in and if there is something that is unpleasant or is disrupting the group you may use your sword on that individual around their energy field and cut from them their connection to whatever this evil source is.'

'I am reading a book on mystics and I am very drawn to Morgan in the Mists of Avalon. Can you tell me something about my connection with her?'

'You were her my dear.'

'What did I not get then that I can do now?'

'Then it was a kind of inquisition going on in Spain. There was much trouble, there were killings, there were religious wars, there was an extreme dominance of Catholic beliefs and cruelty that went on at that time. There were still Moslems that were being sacrificed literally, bloodbaths that were taking place, and what it was to you was so overwhelmingly shocking and something you could not conceive of and you could not try to convince them that that was the wrong way because it shocked you in your entire being. They were killing the lambs. They were sacrificing them, bringing in blood where there needed to be prayer and worship and it tended to paralyse you at that time. You did not find your support system that could have been ambassadors for you who could go out to try and touch those troubled spots, and you did not believe that you had that power. This time you must know you have great powers, my dear; great power is coming through more magnificently than you have ever known in any of your other embodiments. So, all those energies from past lives that you have collectively now recalled will be better instances of those aspects of your personality which will come forward now so that there will not be that fear. You will stand tall and know that you are supporting but in that gentle way. You may deliver the command of the Almighty to those who are to be around you and you will scatter the evil ones that cannot come near you. They will disperse and spread far and wide and they

37

will not try to group against you. They will know that you are so protected and powerful that there is nothing they can do to reach you. That is where you will get a taste of it to begin with and we know and we have looked into your beingness in a very scrutinised way to know that there is no possibility of you running with that power. It is not in your make up, in your cellular being, and we have reinforced in the work that we have been doing on your body that gentleness that yields great power that is so aligned with Spirit, there is not even a consciousness of that old power. You do what you need to do without any qualms saying: "Oh my, I must have destroyed something or I have been unkind". You are to do what Spirit tells you now and carry that message powerfully as the beautiful energy you are. They will see your wings my dear – they will be out there shining much as that angel you have in your room, and they will be in awe.

If you hear that there is no more speaking, a hush in the room, do know and be conscious of what it is they are seeing. You have merely to stand in that light and hold that energy. Do not speak, let it just evolve into what they are hearing and seeing and when you listen, we will tell you when you are to leave the room. It will more likely be towards the end of a group session that no more words are needed. They must see you and feel and witness your beauty. You just remove yourself from the room and the cohort of angels that will be around you will follow you and they will be speechless – that is part of your power – know it, guard it, be a container almost as you would be a basket to hold that energy in your Love and Light and you will be so blessed, my dear, that there will be no thought of: "Look at me, I am powerful" – that will never happen to you, you will carry it with humility and discernment and with those qualities you will know when and how to present yourself in front of a crowd.

It will also come to pass that you will stand on the top of a hill or a mountain and will just stand there in your shimmering beauty without needing to say anything and everyone in the crowd will be touched and feel the message that is being

38

brought to them without any need to give a blessing or honour them or thank them or whatever – just stand up, you might even raise your hand to welcome them and bless them and they will be very silent, waiting for your message and as you do that, the light will blaze in and around you. Much of it will come from the spaceship but it will also be your angels that are shimmering, and, as you stand there holding your arms up, the light will play off your wings and off your golden energy from your crown chakra and they will fall down in tears and cry and be so blessed that they will carry the message to others.'

'That's pretty powerful.'

'It is you who have worked for this and deserved it. It is not that we have decided simply at random that we have chosen you.'

'Oh, I got the long straw or the short straw?'

'The winning straw!'

'Thank you. I've been feeling I want to work with alchemy, like the essences that I have been working with lately that I made. Is that something that I should do or just go through the phase and let it go?'

'Play with it my dear. It is coming as a recreation for you. In other words, it is not just to fall into the TV or into the bead-work or whatever you have been doing – it is an alternative. You will grow so vastly – your entire energy system – so that you will not be satisfied with just one or two paths, you will experiment with this, pick it up, someone else will come by and you will give time to them and then you will go to something else and then you will watch on television some-thing like the fairies or a children's tale about the Isle that is happening within that very programme and be tuning in. Much will attract you now and be as a little child. It is not that you are losing your concentration, on the contrary, you are awakening parts of yourself and saying: "Yes I am alive when I am there and this would be fun to do" – whatever is enjoyable – and know that you carry that energy of the Isle within you. You are not just a keeper of the keys my dear – that could be a burden – and you would stumble along the hallway. Not this time.

So, it will be a light burden and not a heavy one and as you do that you must connect with the group for there you will see the five stars that are around you and you are that central part of the star. You are to check in on each one and connect them to what it is they are needing to do or to align themselves to. You might tell them about their angels or about a spiritual form that is coming to help them evolve in their work and you will be very helpful. You must align them to their Spiritual Guides and more to that energy that is around them that is wanting to express itself through them – not just in the great works that they will do – but also in the lecturing and supporting they will do. Some will do well to stand up in front of business men and explain the work of your group and then answer questions. They may channel and know that they are bringing in the highest of energy. Are there other questions about those six months that you see before you?'

'Well, I had a little bit of fear about being there all by myself.'

'You will never be alone, my dear. I think you know that. To have an animal might be helpful for you – a cat or a dog or whatever you would like – to keep you company. And Mary needs to come as often as possible to be with you and if you call her, she will come immediately. There is much that you two can anchor in and, also, doing your work with the Tibetan energy and bringing those two polarities in and holding them, perhaps, just for a time out in the garden and then walking to different spaces and seeing that you are holding the energy as you are moving. This is important because you will be moving in and out of crowds and then you may ask the fairies to help

40

you to become invisible. They will delight in that. So you can see one another and say: "Do you see me now?", and play at that game which would be great fun for you.'

'Okay, good. I am pretty excited.'

'May I just say one more thing before we conclude your reading, that by August your new body will be essentially visible and it will be refined up until October. So, if you are feeling in pain at times, know that there is much readjustment going on with your joints and with your framework as to how it will hold this new energy. It is almost like a clay model that is being re-touched and modelled according to the way that Spirit would like it to appear. So, some might be working on your inner organs and others will be working on your outer frame and you need to hold your head very high, my dear, so that you will have that noble look again that you have carried in many lifetimes.'

'I almost thought that a lot of my weight problem was about energy; it was about getting this vehicle grounded enough to hold energy.'

'That is in part true and as you walk and you exercise and you are feeling fit again that will help you to ground that energy down. The cells will also be programmed. When Mary works on you she has been informed to ask those cells that are holding any fat content to let it move, to let it go and slip out of your body so that that will be a constant ongoing process for you that you are not aware of, and, as you walk in the air and you walk in nature and are one with it – you might hug trees, you might enjoy the scenery or even imagine standing upon a little knoll or a hill and hold your arms out and let Light and Love and Spirit come to bless you – as long as you are on the ground, it is going to be very healing for you. The more you do it, the faster it will happen. Indian Spirits will come to you.'

'Even in the Isle?'

'Even in the Isle, and you do not need to play with bows and arrows like you did as a child, but that might be a fun project for you at some time. You could bring in young people from the local village in alignment to that energy, that they could play in good fun and you would bring in the energy from your forefathers. Anything more?'

'Is there anything Mary needs at this time?'

'Thank you. She needs to get into her healing again for the more she heals, the more she will be aware of her power which is nothing more than Love and Light coming through her into those she works on and as she sees them blossom, it will warm her heart and she will know that this is part of her path. So, business is business and must be dealt with. Her joy will be more and more in alignment with her work and she must also try to ask for opportunities to work on children and to play with them and also not to neglect her work with channelling trees and fairies and the little ones. If she could have an agenda that at least once a week and once during the weekend, she could connect with that which is part of her work with the elementals. She will find great joy and pleasure in doing it and colour will become very important to her. She will draw with colours on the book that you gave her or she will draw animals or small instances of a star that is particularly brilliant. She may connect to stars as well and may speak about spaceships and clouds – that is allowed to her as well.'

'Thank you. Where are the spaceships coming from that we see over the mountains?'

'Excellent question once again. These are the spaceships that come from a local area. They are coming from a mountain which is located in a straight line as you would fly from here. For example, you would go over that mountain that holds the spaceship energy and they are not always visible. So, if you do see them, know that this is a gift that is given to you. They are on another dimension so they do not have to appear. If they choose to appear, then you are being given a message.'

'I have already seen them three times.'

'So consider it three messages that you have been given – important ones.'

'I was not aware of a message. What did it mean?'

'It was with purpose my dear. It was giving you the message to know that as you are walking the land that you have known in other embodiments that as a North American Indian you will do much to protect the Indians and to align them once again to that energy. You have that power and the other two will merely be enforcing that message.'

'What else could I do to support these Indians?'

'Put it in your journal and refer to it because messages will come to you about that portion of your work, and it might be more books about Indians, it might be meeting them as tribes for there are enlightened beings amongst the North American Indians and you must be selective. Those who go to the casinos and who are spending their time idly are not part of the movement that you will encourage.'

EXPOSÉ ON CHANNELLING

Quan Yin

'I welcome you. As we are gathered together in this most holy place. I welcome those who have never been here before and I say to you that we know each other well. I have been with you often in your meditations, in your channelling group and in your dreams. Sometimes you would not have recognised me for I came in different forms, but you were astute enough – both of you – to recognise that I had another side and that side is what has built the complexity of my energy and my force-field. If I did not have that solid base, that structure that was allowing me to stand in truth alone, in integrity, in the purest of light, I could not carry out the work that I have been doing. Do you see, I stand for no nonsense; there will be none around me and I will not tolerate those devotees who come and bow before me and yet their faces are twisted and their souls are wondering what kind of devilish things they can do.

May I say to you as a group that I am delighted you are here for at last you are finding yourselves and bringing together collectively that energy that I have longed for in this sanctuary. There were others who came and pretended but my perceptions would not allow their masks to come and pretend to worship me. So, now that we are comfortable – and I hope you all are – and thank you for being here and for knowing that this will be a very exciting time for all of you. Do you see, we too have been preparing our agenda and we have good things in mind for you.

There will be teachings from the highest spaces, interfacing with your energies and with this level and lifting you up. At each session, we are doing our utmost to raise your vibrations, your perceptions to open channels within you that have been prepared, faces that you had no idea were filled with knowledge. It is as if you were turning a button on a radio or on some kind of a transistor and you hear another voice, it's another sound and it has other words to say. It will be in the language that everybody understands, but it will be a part of you which you did not know you had. Do you see, we could not release that energy earlier for if we had done so, precious information from the most High would have been delivered into hands that were not pure, that were not washed and did not come as an offering to the Almighty. Now that this has been resolved and you come in your humility, in your love and in your simplicity, we shall see to it that your growth is rapid, that you will be learning things at night, you will come in the morning filled with questions and you will say to yourself: "But I am not the same person I was yesterday; I went to bed feeling thus and such – this morning I am expanded, I feel enlarged, I feel that I can connect with the birds, the trees, with the elements, with the clouds." You are the all that is and you shall become more so knowing where you came from, where you are at present and where you are going. Do you see, that alignment will be so perfect that it will be as if you were squeezing behind a series of mirrors that are juxtaposed so that you don't know whether the image is yourself or someone else. As you wend your way through these passages you will find suddenly that you are not there; you will look down and you have no body; you will look at your hands and they are not there and then you will wonder: "Now where am I to go and where shall I re-appear and how shall I be when I re-appear?" It will be quite terrible and frightening if that were to happen without preparation and we want you to know you shall be prepared; perhaps, not all of you will get into that space, but if you apply yourselves and,

45

especially, those of you who are magicians at heart, you will take the light in surprising your entourage and they will say: "But Daddy was just here – where has he gone?". We don't wish you to make a sideshow out of this and I know you will have greater discretion than that, but you will need this my friends. You will be in crowds where they will be so hungry for your words, for your abilities, for your talents that they will be pulling – not just at your sleeves, or tugging at your wrists or shouting to you – but they will want you; they will want more of you and this one wants you to come with them, the other one says: "No, he's ours. No, we have an appointment with him". Do you see? You cannot be there for all, so that is the time to say "enough is enough" and you will transition and pass into that space, walk right out of the space and go and maybe stand by a tree and ask that you can come back into your normal beingness at which time you will walk away and no one will suspect you were there by the tree.

Sananda did that when he was in India – if you have read the *Nine Faces of Christ* you know when he came to the crowds. They were shouting and some were applauding and others were booing and he was being literally pulled one way and the other. He moved through the crowd without anyone knowing that he was there. Does that sound appealing to you? You would like that? Good, then we shall set that in order. I do believe you have some questions tonight?'

'Mary was wondering – we were all wondering – what more needs to be done to clean up the negativity that may linger at the property?'

'My dears, set your intents of purity, that is all we are asking you. Come to a place that you love and that you cherish and you want nothing more, nothing less. If you see a tree that looks a bit sad you might give it your love. If you see a pebble that you like, pick it up, love it, put it into your pocket and say that you shall put it in a nice place. Be as children – simple at heart, loving every aspect of your morning, your life, open yourselves to the universe, to the fairies, to that which is magical, that which you are longing to be with and that which comes to you. Perhaps, it might be a goose or a duck or it might be a cat that finds you and jumps into your lap. Whatever it is, just love it. At this point you could do some more work on the crystals – that would be very fitting for the crystals cannot reach out to you or tug your sleeve or call to you at night – they will if you focus on them but they are the ones needing your attention and once they are set properly, that they have their auras back, that they are shining, that you can go into them, talk to them, that they will whisper to you at night. Then you will know my friends that all is well, for the crystals truly capture the essence of this sacred ground and of your coming and they are rejoicing within but if they are clouded over and have this negativity surrounding them, there is no way they can reach out to you. So, we would ask you, all of us on our side, please be tender and loving to all but especially to the crystals and I know you are doing just that by turning in to them, by caring for them, lifting out the darkness where you have found it. I for one am extremely grateful. As you can see, I live surrounded by crystals and the ones that are outside, if they are not happy, they will impact on the ones that are around us and wherever you find a crystal, stop and talk to it, cheer it on, help support it. If there are other questions I welcome them?'

'Thinking about the crystals – we were wondering what we can do tomorrow in our services at each crystal to remove the negativity and to help them help us?'

'I do thank you for that question. I would say for the big crystals there would need to be several of you. If it could be all of you, it would be far better. Stand around them, hold hands if you wish, send them your love, however you imagine that love, to go into a crystal in any form. Perhaps you might think of a dear one, someone you have missed or someone you care to see and just send that crystal the love that you would like that one to receive and as you extend your love and the circle grows and it amplifies then, when you feel it properly, you can

47

all go in as someone will give the signal – whoever wishes to – and reach into it and cleanse it as you have done. It is extremely efficacious and something that the crystal responds to beautifully; and then you may raise your hands again as you did over the vortices and just raise your hands up to the heavenly spheres and thank the universe for this golden opportunity to serve.

You are doing magnificently – all of you – and I can only thank you on behalf of the masters, of the angels, the archangels for opening those vortices, opening the portholes, allowing beings to exchange places, allowing energy to flow through this globe and to have such beautiful, responsive and caring beings that you are. It is not enough to say these words; I carry them. Can you imagine them rippling out, much as a stone being thrown into a pond? It is rippling out to the furthest spheres of this galaxy and beyond and they are all delighted. You are making possibilities available to souls who have not had it for many thousands of years and now they are free, they are singing your praises. They are very creative and we do believe when you are back that you will find changes. They would like your interaction wherever you may be, so you may talk to them and you may refer to them as the lightbeings at the sacred Island who come from the planet Riegel – however you choose to pronounce it.

It is a very sacred space and these beings have taken on a task which is not an easy one; they have come to help in the transition as you go into the photon belt. So, the more you fortify them, the more love you send them, the more you strengthen them the better they can do their work and you will find that those areas that you are in where the vortices are, where your centres are set up, they are doing everything to see that the weather shall be stabilised, that there be a protective ring around those areas so that the energy will be softened as it comes in. You will not have a jagged edge or a storm or a pocket of energy that is so negative it splits off from an island, or that parts of it drop into the sea or whatever else could happen. If you will note as you look, certain islands that are in those waters are being charged. That is what the dolphins and the whales are doing and they are setting up an energy field which is responding very much to the crystals. Their sensors are capturing the sound waves coming from the crystals and they are building a protective area around it so that many fish and many parts of the marine life will take shelter in those waters.

There are space centres deep down into the inside of the workings underneath these islands. Much is going on. I do not want to give you all the picture, but I want you to know that come August you will have some dramatic events happening in and around these islands, and, perhaps, some are good, perhaps some are not so good, but you will start noticing the spaceships. If you are there in September when the violence has calmed down, you will be invited on board and you might expect to go up and away, but you might go down and below, and it will be equally exciting, so do not feel that the fun has left you somewhere abandoned and you have not been able to enjoy your turn in a ship. I am getting beyond my story. I am sorry. What else can I do?'

'Can we put stones from other places around the crystals?'

'Very helpful my dear. For example, it would give much encouragement to the big crystal which is up on this hill here and the other one which is indeed suffering. If you bring that in, you will find them all beginning to connect and align and there will be a response, if you could imagine much activity going on for they do connect and they will be very happy.'

'I have another question about the crystal in the wooden crate near the entrance – it appears to be misplaced. Where should it be?'

'Indeed. Thank you. It is waiting to find its place and you could all talk to it and surround that one with a great deal of love. It has been abandoned, it was in the sunshine, had a family around it and the family left and it was bereft and grieving and no one noticed it was in the dark. It had no sunshine, no light and it shut down. So, there is a place. It has been out in the sun now for some time and had time to settle down, so if you are kind enough to connect into its energy and ask would it like to be in a sunny place, would it like to be up high, would it like to be near plants, what is it longing to do and what is its role here? It has a very specific one but I would prefer that it would tell you so.'

'Could you tell us please how the small crystal outside the learning centre is doing?'

'It is probably one of your more powerful crystals here and it was not sure it wanted to stay here for some moments now.'

'Would you be able to offer us guidance on what the Higher Self of the Learning Centre in the Isle needs?'

'That is a tall subject, my dear. There are many aspects in such, how can I say, ancient places as the Isle. It has the old energy from the Druids, from the Celts, from the Mannanin energy which, of course, was space-beings who nurtured land starting from that point and working down into the continent and down into Italy, so it gave an impetus – if you can imagine a renaissance – starting somewhere. It started in those waters off the Isle, so you have so much attachment to stories of fairies, of Druids, but also you have the spaceships interacting there. Then you have the local folklore of fine people who had gone underground and they had their own Guides and Gods and you have the Ladies of the Lake, you have King Arthur, Merlin; all of that energy has been interspersed with what we would say was pure intent of the Isle. Can you imagine, dear sir, one of those keys that you have picked up among the rocks and found the key and you are looking for the other stone that will go with it – the Isle is the key – do you see that? And you my dears are bringing the stones to the key. So, it is a powerful space, it has much energy. It has ancient and hidden energy that no one has even tapped into or believed in, but it is not able to awaken until you are bringing the stones to the keys.

50

You are gathering them, you are bringing them in, you will start this whole process and, as it takes on momentum and it becomes powerful and people recognise the power, they will try to imitate you and that is the time when we will ask you to change and shift and go into something entirely different. I don't want to deal with that right now because you have enough on your plates – each and every one of you. Part of your intent as you gather here will be to see where you are coming from – are you a Druid, are you someone with magical energy like Merlin or are you someone who lived in a cave? What was your intent when you first came to the Isle? I do believe you all recognise you have been there in past lives. So, when you connect with that part of you, and your friends will help you, it would be best if you could all tune in to it beforehand. Once you come up with that piece, you will know what type of individual you will attract and what you will offer them that will intrigue and fascinate and be as something they crave: a chocolate that they are desiring so desperately. They will come to your centre not knowing why they are there, but because of something you said or because of your energy and they say: "Yes, that's something I need". What they don't realise is they are coming to connect with that part of them that has been there before, has done this work, knows this and has very little to do in order to learn it. So, once you have found the major pieces, then it will go really very smoothly and you will be surprised how quickly these people will learn, how decisive they will be; they will not hesitate in front of danger or threats. They will go right to the bookshelf and pull down the right information, the important book, whatever it is they want, but you will be providing the space, the energy, the openness for them to choose. Is that something you understand? Have you more questions? I truly welcome them right now.'

'We have another question about other locations. I know you said for us not to think about a lot of new things at this point, but just to get in our mind's eye what other location we may be needing to focus on down the line?'

51

'I would say at the moment it is best to concentrate on the Isle, for if you do get dispersed you will think about that and then you will wonder: "Well, what will I do there?", or "What kind of people will come?", or "I don't speak Spanish", or you will imagine a thousand hurdles. We would like you to see it going to the point where you feel comfortable – each one of you – that you have found that which you really long to do and that awakens something in you, that there is a piece that says: "I know this; I know I can do a good job". You will have no doubts when you have found it and you will not have to say, "Oh help, I do not speak well in front of people", or "I would be embarrassed to show them something I really don't think I know", and all those doubts will be dispelled. By the time you leave here, I do believe each one of you will have that key that you are needing.'

'Mary wants to know what is happening to her energy fields?'

'Well, I would say this is not just for Mary. I would say at this point in time you can expect almost anything. We would not suggest you drive very far in these vehicles for you might suddenly become dizzy and you might say: "I am nauseous", or "I am seeing double and I am wondering what is happening to me". It will happen within the next three days that you will go through a transition. It's as if you are walking behind that mirror but you still see parts of yourself, you are still conscious of being in your body, but you don't know quite where you need to go or where you want to go. Your minds will be stilled because you are not supposed to think about this – just let it happen. We would not like you to be carrying a tray of water for example or something more dangerous, so you would slip and fall and have an accident. We do like to think that you would be sitting down or, if it comes about quickly, find a place to sit and manage just to let it happen. This is the time to let it happen. You have cleansed the house. You have done the very best to see to it that we are all safe in our energy, that we have no outside influences that are going to impact us and now let go – breathe, allow it to come in through your crown chakras, through your heart – however you choose to breathe – but breathe in that love, breathe in the energy; let it out to say: "Yes I want it, please give me that peace that I am to know about", and then you might want to share it with others. It will be quite exciting. In fact, if you wake up at night and wonder where you are, you might not find the right direction, so perhaps you would all like a little night light or a small pocket light to remind you that you are in a strange place. You might feel a little awkward or dizzy or say: "I am not sure quite which direction the bathroom is". I think you will find it, but I am just giving this as an example.

At any rate we want you to be cheerful and to know that this is all in great fun. We will not bring in elves or other beings who bump into you or you might find yourself face to face with them. That would not be in divine order right now. It is to allow yourselves to go in and out of dimensions. Now you will do this for others. So, please, if you could take notes and keep journals, remember precisely how it felt – whether you were confused, whether you were worried, were you afraid, what was the emotion that you were feeling at that time, was there anything that carried through after the experience and would you say to yourself: "Oh, I wouldn't want to go through that again", or "Oh, this was exciting – when can it happen to me again?", and it will happen again but not quite the same way. So, be free, be open, share with one another. It might be very dynamic, you might see your lights again, you might suddenly have the fireplace light up, you might see something outside which is a strange light – it will be somehow magical like you have known in your childhood. So, be prepared. It shall be a joy and you will be able to introduce the others to it when they arrive. Are there other questions my dears?'

'Would you give us some recommendations on how we, as individuals, can gain our power back?'

'That will be the main theme of this group meeting when you will be starting your symposium, if that is the proper

53

word. Your facilitator will allow you to feel instances where you have experienced your power – what was it that felt very good? Was it because you were powerful and people were looking to you for that extra piece? Was it a moment of victory over something very difficult? Was it an ego that was expressing itself through you saying: "I am better than others – look, I have just proved it". What does power mean to each one of you? Do you see where you have left it behind in a moment when you erred? There was a mistake that happened, but it was just an experience. It was not meant to be left with you forever, much as a tattoo might be left on your body, as a scar – this you have carried with you in different aspects from lifetime to lifetime. You have regained aspects of your power and you have lost it again. You have been humble and allowed things to happen and then, receiving from Spirit, your power came back to you without knowing it. You have chosen ways in which to express your power.

You see, there is so much that is intricate around this issue of power. What is power after all? It is nothing more than the divine that is coming through you. You have opened yourselves so completely to the love, to the light, to Spirit, to allow anything that Spirit would let happen to come through. You have walked with Spirit, you've talked with Spirit. May I say it may be expressed as your Higher Self, you love your Higher Self so much that it is allowing it to come in freely. You are walking in bliss. Your Higher Self is expressing herself/himself through you; you are doing nothing and then, at that moment you are in your power and you are not even aware of it, my dears, that is real power. It will happen as you release and you allow yourselves to move in and out of these dimensions. You will be playful, perhaps little elves and fairies will be beside you and you will be laughing, sitting outside near a tree laughing – no one knows why – but you are releasing, you are letting go. You are playing as you did as a child – it's meant to be fun. We will be there for you, I assure you, to reassure you that you are not crazy.'

'What needs to be done to join all the crystals that have been placed in different locations? What needs to be done to join them all together?'

'Very good and I thank you for a closing message, this is beautiful. It merely means your love is tying them all together – nothing more. They feel it from each one of you, they know it, they expand, they grow. The others are feeling it on the Isle and there is a very powerful one that is about to be set into action and you all will feel it if you tune in to it. It is too soon yet, but as you can think of these crystals, you are helping them tie together. We have asked some of you to try and remember the crystals on the vortices, especially the portholes at night, before you go to bed – sing them a song and just say "Goodnight, little ones", let anything happen that can happen and in the morning, when you bring the Sun into your being- ness and you welcome it, allow it to pass through you into those crystals. So, bring the light into them, think of them, love them. Tell them they are your family for they are working very well for you; each one is serving a very noble and other dimensional service. They have come from Atlantis many of them, others have been brought from the Pleiades, some have come from Sirius and there are others that have been meteors that have fallen onto your ground, your land, and have come to you by magic but, as you know, there is no such thing as just magic – there is an intent that it comes to the right source. So, bring your love in wherever you are, walk with that love, see that love, stand for the love and as you look at my statue which is alive as I am here with you, let our hearts connect and let our Higher Selves come in and greet one another. With that I wish you a pleasant evening, that you will enjoy the energy. It might be perhaps a ride, it might be eating marshmallows by a campfire and it might be just wonderfully good fun. So, I leave you with my love and the blessings that are coming to you from so far and wide, that all these beings are gathering around to speak to you, to feel you, to touch you, to enlighten you as you would imagine a bonfire being lit. It will happen in your midst and it will be mingled with the Violet Rays from St Germain. It will be many energies and many forces and much power as you feel it, connect to it, live with it and ask it to purify you and help you set your intent for this group meeting. We are with you and we pray for you. We leave you in Love and Light and say thank you for coming. Adonai.'

BEING STRONG AND GUIDED
BY THE LIGHT

St George

'I send you my love and thanks for coming here on such a wonderful day when you could all be doing something else and rather be doing something else with your privileged time. Thank you for coming here and sharing your energy.'

'Thank you St George. I have a question involving anything that we might need to know concerning the group – I mean the group of all of those beautiful souls who are wanting to start the healing centres as we are trying to group together. Do you have any counselling for us or advice?'

'That is a very wise question. Dear ones, it is so simple. All those that actually group together, unite together, should live and breathe the same air as everyone does on this planet Earth, so why not share your wonderful thoughts, your wonderful ideas, your vision. What would you like to see of this group, how would you like to see yourself involved with this group – which part, which role are you going to play? Once you find yourself on this level of energy, let no one hold you back, but just walk forward and you know it. You are strong and the light will guide you and there will not be any dark forces to hold you back. There will be a little negative energy and it is coming through individually but you will find these are earth beings not humans. So, the only advice I can give you is to

57

hold on to that goal in your heart. Any decision that you make must come from your heart at all times and never let your ego take control. Let your heart, your lighter side, light up. laugh, enjoy what you are doing or what you are about to do. It is so important that you do these from the bottom of your heart, that all your thoughts and all of your energy comes from it. If you follow through there is nothing there to stop you.

As for any project, I beg you, go all the way through and even though there is going to be a lot of negativity around you, by all means, do not let it bother you in any way or hold you back or change what you are planning to do. Do not let anyone scare you in that matter. Have faith and ask for guidance for any wisdom to come up and above you and pray that those that you have put all your trust in follow through with their words and it would be a great idea if perhaps some of that group, the people that you will be dealing with, would just, at the time that the meeting will occur, send a prayer and love and some light in the beginning and at the end.'

'Beautiful St George. I don't know if there is anything else to say. If anyone comes to us saying you have no right to do this – do we still stand firm at all costs?'

'Indeed dear one. Who are they to tell you that you have no rights? They could try to manipulate you but don't let that happen to you. Let your advisors and legal source deal with that matter. They will find the best way and they will deal with it correctly and properly and eventually you will be smiling and happy – the way life should be in a spiritual level – there should not be disruption going on. Those around you, not just you, are going through a big test but, by all means, this test will follow through and should be a lesson to all concerned that you all can succeed in doing what is right.'

'Thank you St George. I was told that I am going through a transition right now with this beautiful Angel Goddess,

58

Elizabeth, who is coming to me to assist me in this process. Is there anything I need to do particularly at this time?'

'Just give it up, give yourself up and let Spirit guide you through. You are so lit up now you have actually released all the negative energies that have been attached to you. At the moment, just walk on that air and let them guide you through. Love them the same way you have loved those around you and you shall see the tremendous changes – not just in your energy level – but in your Light Being.'

'And in my memory?'

'If you knew what they were doing to you, you would not just be smiling but singing away happily.'

'Thank you St George. And I was told to use Excalibur if I am feeling any doubts. Is that correct?'

'Doubts dear one? Why? You can use it but the doubts come with fear. If you let fear go the doubts will go. So, please dear one, have no fear. Only those that walk with fear attract the darkness. Walk lightly and have trust in our Holy Father and he will remove any fear or doubts that you have.'

'Thank you and what blessed words you have given me. Such hope and encouragement. I thank you St George.'

'So much advice that one can give or how much. Dear one, in which way would you rather go? You can either go with the light or stay. By staying, you will not accomplish anything. There is only one way to go and that is forward. Seek that wonderful light that shines – it could be a star, it could be the sun but go forward and don't let anyone hold you back in any way. After all, you are a free Spirit, you are a gift from our Holy Father and why not use it?'

'Thank you.'

'St George, any advice for me?'

'This is beginning to sound like a class. I am not a great teacher but I would be glad to help those who actually ask for my help. Advice to you, dear one, is courage and you have gone a long way. Now it is time to bring all those wonderful ideas and thoughts and energy forward to the people that you are dealing with on a daily basis. Use your knowledge, use your healing skills and by giving that wonderful knowledge and that wonderful healing, you are actually healing yourself. This advice is for all of you in this wonderful chapel. You have all been so connected together, so why don't you share your wonderful energy and ideas together and be united as one. That's the wonderful advice that I can give to everyone that comes to this beautiful energy – to share your thoughts, your ideas, your gifts that you bring, share them together, unite together and you shall see them grow tremendously. It is like a crystal – so little, but when the sun shines, it glows and it grows as that energy expands and goes further and further away, that wonderful energy that you all brought together – it grows with you all.'

'Thank you.'

'And dear ones, if you don't have other questions for now, I would like instead of you thanking me, dear ones, to thank the Holy Father for being here together, united and sharing your wonderful thoughts and ideas. May that wonderful light always shine brighter and brighter as you get one step closer to your dreams and wonderful goals. Amen.'

HOW AND WHEN TO ASK FOR HELP

Archangel Michael

'I am Archangel Michael. This is a different setting than we have had before, but it is perhaps more comfortable for both of you than sitting in the bathtub. I enjoy our chats whenever and wherever we may have them and find that you too are, in your closeness, bringing a magnificent energy onto this globe. You do not measure it in the same terms as we do. You think you are carrying on your daily preoccupations, but I say to you that you are doing far more than you have any idea of and may that warm your hearts and help to somehow allay the tribulations and the weight of the burdens you are taking on. So many tend to use this experience, if you will, as an excuse to do things that are less pleasant for them but we have not found that to be the case for either one of you. You carry on diligently what you have set out to do – whether you are feeling up to it or not – and these energies that we send to you are to reinforce you, to help support you, certainly to protect you and to make it easier for you both to carry on your tasks. Hence we are also supplying you with some interesting information coming through your craving for books and knowledge and to understand better where you are.

Tonight I would like, first of all, to say that my purpose of being here is to help you both, to clear up any misgivings or perhaps difficulties you are having or explain to you where you are and it is also coming with the intent of surrounding

61

you both with my energy and my love. I do know it is difficult and we have heard it from other earth beings who have evolved into our spiritual realm saying how much they felt alone and disconnected from humans and from Spirit at times which made their task very arduous and perhaps more difficult than climbing a mountain peak such as the Himalayas. There the wind would be blowing and your fingers would be freezing, your toes about to fall off and you say: "Why am I doing this and what is my purpose?". So, we have agreed amongst us, the Ascended Masters, the other angels and archangels who are working with you, that we need to come in more often at periods that will be compatible with you and answer your questions. Also, we want to tell you how much we value you, your work, your personalities, your diligence and your devotion. It is very similar to the kind of energy that Sananda carried at the time when he was evolving against, I could say "overwhelming", burdens, disparity and negativity. You have nowhere to gain support or guidance outside of yourselves and your own connection with us. So, once again, I repeat that we do want you to be with us as much as possible and to ask, even to let yourselves cry if that is necessary, to express emotion to one another or to us in asking how best we can help you at this time. It is a critical time for both of you. So do you have questions, my dears?'

'Yes I do. I have some written and some not written, but we'll start with the written ones. Mary is going through a process here where she is merging one being into another being. Can you tell her something about this being? How would you describe her?'

'I am glad you asked my dear. Actually, she comes from Sirius and we have withheld that knowledge from Mary for she did not need to rush to a book to have some preconceived idea of what a being would be like from Sirius. This is a being who has not only offered to help us at this moment, but who has also been connected with the channel. They have worked together on other assignments out in – not just your galaxy –

62

but in other universes. So, they think in similar ways and they undertake tasks with the same amount of devotion and application and this being is someone who has a sense of her role in this growth of your planet as being instrumental for she carried many secrets, but to her they are only keys to living and ways in which people can feel at ease in collaborating. She says: "They need to share in your joy and enthusiasm" without you having to rush out and say: "Please, I have something I need to tell you and you must hear me and I need to heal you". That would not serve your purpose well and it is not a spell that she casts upon people, but she has a way of intriguing others and being a very warm and compassionate soul. She does know how to interact with individuals as well as groups and she is very discerning as to who is there to be supportive of the group and of her or his own energy and those who are coming out of curiosity or pretending to be part of it – much as a newspaper reporter might agree to come into a group so that he or she might get a scoop, an article that would pay rich dividends. She will immediately rip the mask off such entities so that you may be very clear as to who you are dealing with and if she allows them in, then you know that these are people who will work with you eventually.'

'Okay. Is she a being that has been attached to Mary through all times?'

'No my dear. That is an astute question, but she comes and she goes into this other state. She has another way of becoming a shape shifter and you could not recognise her. If I may use as a reference the film *Cocoon* – I do not remember whether it was *Cocoon* or *Cocoon 2*, but in that film you saw a Light Being looking like a very beautiful and glamorous Earth model and when she took her suit off she became a shimmering light, totally different with no size to her, no definite shape. You could not even recognise her as a face and a body, legs and arms. So this being has that ability to become either totally a Light Being or to become invisible if that is required. Also, she can project herself to a spaceship or even back to

Sirius if it is needed. That is a more complicated and involved, as well as evolved, journey and she has tried to put aside her other work for this commitment so that she would be totally available to both of you.'

'Okay. So could we say that this being holds the potential of Mary's Light Being?'

'Put it this way, Mary is not aware in her present state of that desire or commitment, but that is accurate and they have great similarities in their DNA, in their cellular structure. That is why we have had to do a crash course, if you will, on Mary because this soul was ready and Mary was not so we could not delay one nor the other; we had to speed up everything and as it was described to you this morning I believe in your automatic handwriting, that you are now going at a faster ratio compared to the other beings. If we could put you on a race track, you would already be off this Earth compared to the others who would be progressing as perhaps ants or small bunny rabbits.

When they merge, it will be a joint collaboration to the extent that sometimes even you my dear will be confused as to whom you are speaking. If there is a need to be clear and you have a problem with this amalgamation, you might ask them to distinguish themselves when they speak to you and that will be their love and respect for you.'

'And her name?'

'Her name I cannot give you, my dear, for she does not want to be known by that.'

'Is there something that I can know her by so that when I ask which one it is I can say is this Mary or is this – just any name or something that she might like to be known by if she doesn't want her real name to be given?'

'The name I am being given, and this is for me, as well, is

Alta and it is spelt as it sounds. You may ask: "Am I speaking to Alta or am I speaking to Mary?"'

'You may have already answered this for me but what is her purpose and what does she want to accomplish?'

'Excuse me my dear, there are other entities outside, you might want to shut the door temporarily.'

'What is her purpose, Alta's purpose, and what does she need from Mary? You may have already answered that.'

'I would reiterate strongly that her purpose is to change the energy on this Earth and it was only possible to make that decision when she knew that both of you were working with all of your strength and all of your beingness to cleanse the astral level, for that was her big concern in accepting this task.'

'Okay, thank you. Is there anything that Mary needs to know about taking care of herself during the rest of this integration process?'

'I am wanting to say to her to rest more but I believe she is understanding that and she may do the work that you are already involved in in the morning, but I would like to insist that she has a rest after lunch.'

'Every day?'

'Every day, yes. And she may reappear at 2.30 or 4.00 – whatever is appropriate and the evenings are still very long and bright so she may enjoy an evening outing with you by car, by bicycle – whatever you wish to do – and swimming would be extremely good for her, so please insist.'

'What about body functions for her? Is there something that she needs to change about her diet?'

'That was simply temporary. Alta could not come into a body that was filled with negative particles – it needs to be a major cleansing.'

'So she is establishing her routine once again. There are certain foods she must be careful about: too much pasta would not be a good idea and if she could stay away from chocolate for the time being. I believe if she gets into rice cakes, that will satisfy that gnawing hunger that she has.'

'Before we move on to another subject, is there anything else that you need to say for Mary?'

'She knows now that Alta comes every evening and that she will not speak but will explore the body and they will come to an agreement as Mary might ask if she is willing to speak to her. For the moment there is no interaction in terms of words, though she hears everything Mary says to her and has acknowledged the warm welcome she has received. It is also a difficult task for her so there must be respect around, not having telephones ringing at night or an alarm going off. It is principally at the time when Mary goes to bed that she will integrate her energy and will stay until sometimes 2.00 in the morning getting familiar with this body and how it functions and the mind set particularly, so that the two may work in perfect synchronicity and not have one pulling in one direction and the other one being emotionally needy so that there is not an understanding. It's like talking to somebody who is totally mental and the other is very abused emotionally – you do not know what happens in that exchange.'

'Thank you. I am just sitting here looking at Alta and I get this sea coloured green around her which I picked up the other day.'

'If you were asked to describe her to Mary you would say she has a very regal bearing about her and green is her colour;

it was the colour of her eyes. Now, it has been decided that if Mary were to change the colour of her eyes, no one apart from you would recognise her and that would not be satisfactory. She must not at this moment disconnect totally from her family but there will be times when you are speaking to crowds and there are moments when her eyes will change to that beautiful green.'

'Is her hair colour different as well?'

'She has a reddish tint to her hair. It is not flaming red as you would call it, it is a light auburn shade. You shall have something similar my dear so do not envy her.'

'On the 17th we are being asked to open a vortex in one of the fields. We ask, with respect, if there are any instructions?'

'Yes, proceed, as usual, with your individual prayers and blessing. Raise your arms in welcome and return to the four corners. Hold the energy and observe. The ceremony will have Alta present and what you set forth and what comes from your hearts and your souls and your desires will be magnified by her. She is a key personality in this growth episode and has accepted her role as allowing it to, ripple – if you could imagine a stone being thrown into a pond and there you would have ripples forming in circular waves around that pebble – she is actually dispersing that energy in rays that will shoot forth from this centre. It will come from the spaceships but it will also be distributed out over the land as far as the eastern coast of the UK, of England and Scotland to the western coast of Ireland.

So, it will have enormous ramifications and you will be asked to draw on all of your love and your compassion – not just for the Mother Earth crystal – but also for this globe, for if you are present, the three of you, it is because of your love of this planet and of not wanting to see it destroyed. You are asking to play a critical role at key moments.'

'So is there anything else we need to know about the ceremony?'

'I would say that you will see when you open the porthole a blue vibrating shaft of light as we described once before will come down into the ground, but you must pull it down with your energy, not as if you are pulling to hang on to it, but just to anchor it. It will contain you four and this is a very big happening for all of you. You will find your energy fields changed after that, you will be connected directly to that spaceship and it is Commander Mendezar's spaceship that is doing this work for you. As you bring it in and anchor it to the ground, it will pierce through the entire globe but it will also set up a similar vibration on the other side of the globe – it is that powerful, my dears. So, if your energy is a bit affected you might be having spasms as Mary is at present because her energy ratio is so high tonight that she is not able to contain it all, and you will, also, have similar experiences.'

'Will we be guided to know more about the photon image?'

'Yes my dear. I believe I did not fully answer your last question. There was a concern about being given an adjustment in the auric field of certain beings and that was what was meant. You will see it as a blinking light, it may be a colour, it may just be a frequency that attracts your eye; one of your eyes might pick it up. There may be an auric field, something that is almost flashing at you and it will vary as to its texture or colour or size, but when you see that you will know that is your indication and you will try to bring that blue light down over the person and grind them into the ground. That will establish their commitment to serve as well.'

'Are there other ceremonies or openings we need to prepare for?'

'Not to worry further, my dear, for you have so much on

68

your plate that it is not imminent, it will not come before another seven to eight months and in that time period when you will have evolved to your full beingness, Mary, as well, you will be acting differently, thinking differently. You could be representing another planet or a sun energy or even a sun and moon energy together. So, you will be different beings and if I was to tell you you will react in such a way and you will carry such a message – it would not be accurate. We are even observing your change and quite marvelling at what it is doing and how it is affecting your beingness and the light that you carry.'

'Can you explain where we are in our dying or releasing process?'

'If I was to say it on a measuring tape, for example if you have a measuring tape with sixty feet on it, I would say you are both at forty-five feet – you are more than halfway. It means there will be more pain, there will be necessarily more periods of malfunctioning of body parts or just a total relapse of your body energy. I know, my dear, that that is painful for you to hear because you have been through so much so we are very sorry, but as Alta comes in she will know more how to adjust your energy and to be there for you as much as possible. We want you and Mary to be as close as you can for you will know how to support one another because you understand who she is and she because she will know what to do and can even anticipate things before they happen – for example your thyroid – she will sense that before it happens.'

'Mary and I did some channelling last week and when I began to channel there was an excessive amount of noise, it sounded like wind or static or something like that. What is that?'

'My dear, as you open up to channel and to receive what you think is one being, you have that capability of opening yourself up to many dimensions. So what you are getting is static as if it were an antennae that was going literally off the globe. You have that unique ability so your channelling will not always be as clear as you would like it to be and for many reasons. That is why sometimes we prefer the automatic handwriting; you do that extremely well and there is no need to worry about it, you just have such a capability of going in and out of these dimensions that you carry that energy with you and it does tend to crowd things. Others wonder why when they have asked you a simple question why does it have to have this nuisance noise.'

'Thank you, that helps explain that. I guess the other thing I would like to ask is since Mary gets Alta, who do I get? You said I could have one too!'

'I am not sure whether you are ready to handle it yet my dear. You will receive your twin soul and I would like to say more but I think at this time I will just let the intrigue speak for itself. I am not prepared at this moment to allude to that, it might upset you or set you to worry or imagine when it begins to start and you are feeling the process, share it please with Alta and Mary and they will be able to assist you at that time with the information you are needing.'

'Thank you. Well that's all the questions I have. Is there anything else you need to talk to us about?'

'Your energy, my dear, is very much attached to Andromeda and any books you might find on that subject or any writers who deal with it or even an encyclopaedia might give you some tips as to what kind of energy it might be and what to expect. It is very similar to the planeterra and you will be very much at home there. At times its beauty does not equal this and at other times it is overwhelmingly vast and wondrous and you will feel very comfortable there, and you will know how to introduce others to that energy. You will not just be a princess but a queen of Andromeda and will be greatly honoured and revered and listened to. So, you will have a learning process with your twin soul as to what you have been working on in many past lifetimes and that the purpose of those lifetimes was to bring you to this point. It is nothing compared to what you do when you are out of body, in other dimensions, in other universes I do grant you that but it is a large portion of what your lifetimes on Earth have represented. They have been a stepping stone because you will be able to draw on all of those lifetimes and know how it felt when this happened or what was needed at that time that no one understood. For example, as you saw in the theatre last night, and you knew instantly what was needed and how the situation could be corrected to make a magnificent display and a far more exciting drama so also you shall be very good at that like a theatre director, if you will, for the new life that will unfold. Mary and Alta will be teachers in that domain.'

'I would like to ask some questions.'

'Yes.'

'What can we do to help our dear friend who is visiting now? At present she is feeling very, very insecure and lonely and kind of out of touch.'

'If you could imagine, my dear, a child who has fallen off his or her bicycle and is badly bruised. The child is hurt and does not understand why he or she is hurt, wants to cry yet wants to be strong and brave and cannot cry. She is needing to cry, my dear, and if there is some way that you could bring her to that state, whether it is a loving arm about her shoulders or asking her just to sit down and hold your hands, or if it would be better for one to do it and then another; not that both of you do it at the same time. She might not understand that, but she is needing to be touched. It's the child who never got the affection nor the attention and the stress level is responsible. I would say she is very devoted to both of you and wants to serve you well, but she needs that contact. It's as if it's

71

continual reassurance that she is looking for and her neediness will begin to dwindle and become less demanding on you both.

If you give her the time when you are feeling her; just allow yourselves to tune in to her energy and when you are feeling that need give her a call, reassure her. She is a very good person and, as you will see when she unfolds, it will be magnificent. She is one of the powerful leaders of the planet and has great knowledge, but she has been fighting her evolution and not wanting to become that being for fear that again she would be left out and be a cast out. So, she needs a great deal of reassurance; I would say to you, perhaps, to do some emotional work with her in the sense that she will remember it. Pray that your energy will come through clearly. She needs constantly to be reassured.'

'Anything else?'

'No, not unless you have something you want to say to us?'

'I would like to speak about your soul journey my dear for you probably wonder at night where it is you are going, what you are doing as if to say who is the mastermind who is deciding where I shall go next and what particular task I shall undertake. It is applicable for both of you because you offer so generously "I'll do this" and the other says, "No, I'll do it" and then the task is divided between you often, and you do have other attributes that are going to be needed from us. We have found replacements for you to work on the astral belt and that it will not have to always include you and drain you as it has, so that you will in that sense feel an enlightening in your energy level, but we are going to ask you to go further out beyond this universe into a place you know very well. Both of you have been there and there is a task that is needing to be done in that particular space and it will stretch you out to the extent that you will need to go to bed – not too late. If you could perhaps be in bed with the lights out by 10.30. This may

72

be demanding and uncomfortable for you, my dear, but it will be necessary otherwise we are afraid that your lymph glands and your general health will be drawn down. It will only take place for about ten days but both of you will be going through it and so you might compare notes the next morning. If you could retain something or ask before you go to sleep that you might remember an aspect of it and take notes – you will be very interested to know what you are doing.'

'Can I ask you about a person?'

'Yes.'

'The first person I would like to ask you about is an associate who first channelled you for me many years ago – is she evolving into where she needs to be and is she going to be doing what she calls her "Spirit work" soon?'

'My dear, she needs your assistance. She is not evolving as she needs to and she has taken another – well, she has been "distracted" if I may say it that way. She has been pulled into another area which is not her area of expertise nor is it allowing her to open up fully to her beingness as one of our major key people upon this Earth. Because she is getting distracted and pulled away from her source, we cannot pull her back if she does not listen to us any longer and this is very worrisome. Thank you for being concerned.'

'Is she one of the ones who eventually down the road could be healed at the Isle?'

'Yes, and she will bring many in to be healed as she gets healed. Her gratitude is such that she will cry a great deal, recognising that she has made a mistake but you may underline at that time it was no mistake – it was just a lesson.'

'And then will she be able to go out and teach?'

'Indeed. She will teach even new things that she has no idea of.'

'Thank you. I would like to ask about another acquaintance.'

'What would you like to know?'

'About her growth and is she going through what Mary and I are going through?'

'She needs you, my dear. It's as if you anchor her and her energy and her purpose. When she is not with you she does not find that spiritual companionship that she needs for her evolvement. So, if there was a way that you could perhaps take a holiday from the Isle and be with her or sometime that she could come back here with you or to take a trip or somehow manage to spend more time with her, that you could see more clearly what it is that she does that defeats her purpose. She becomes distracted and material things take on a greater importance than they need to at this moment and it is fracturing her energy field. So, at one time she may be very committed and very directed towards her goal and at other times one side of her is pulling in one direction and the other is pulling in another and she is in the middle, not knowing where to go.'

'So, it would be very healing for her to be at the Learning Centre in the Isle when she comes?'

'Very much so and get her to get in touch with the crystals. She will hear from the crystals and they will speak to her. She will get great guidance while she is here. She needs to go out into the glen and experience the glens, the fairies. Whatever she is attracted to, she must do, and you will find the time, I know, to be with her and to accompany her and let her speak. Let her cry, my dear; she has not done much of that in her lifetime.'

'Are there subtle bodies that need to be worked on?'

'For her emotional make up could block her reacting with more clarity to a situation and I believe that you will know how to recognise where she is and help her and Mary could be of some help to her. They will find great companionship and recognise they have been sisters in a past life.'

'Thank you.'

'And I thank you my dear and I wish you a lovely evening. I am sure you have another book to intrigue you but perhaps try to remember the 10.30 deadline if you could. I thank you and I leave you. We shall be with you always, my dears, and you must know that in your business meetings, or whatever affairs you are involved in at this point are only a prelude of what you are going to do later on. So, we are present in this prelude so that everything will be laid, the groundwork will be laid, the stepping stones will be there in their place and you will know when the time comes how to follow the path that we are laying for you.'

'Thank you, that feels good.'

'So, I leave you my dear with the blessings of the Holy Spirit and from Sananda, especially, his love and his gift of support and guidance and to tell you that he is always there for both of you and not to be dismayed if he does not come, that you may always call upon him and he hears you and so do I. With love and respect and the greatest of blessings that can shine upon this Earth, I leave you and anxiously await our coming together again very soon.'

* * *

'I greet you my friends. I am Archangel Michael. I have come to feel your companionship, the softness of your energy and, may I say, a family gathering for I am not alone. You might have guessed that I have friends who flutter in and out and they are angels and Archangel Gabriel is here with me and Archangel Uriel and also Sananda and I believe that is a special blessing to all of us – myself included. I wish to be of help to you and at the same time to allow yourselves to feel the beauty and the peace of this gathering, of this place, of the heaven sent blessings that are coming to you from so many directions, from so many souls, from the Earth itself; that the trees are reaching out to you, that there is warmth, the animals are performing for you, the little birds are laying eggs for you and all of it you might say is just nature's way of expressing itself. But I say to you it is expressing in the fullness of its blossoms and its blooms; everything that could be enhanced is and you shall notice it in the foliage, the trees, the lighting, the greens. Remark to one another when you do notice it, when it strikes you, so that you may appreciate it and see it through each other's eyes.

There is much that is happening, my dears, on many, many subtle levels and from the highest realms that are penetrating far closer and deeper into this Earth than could happen before simply because the light is allowed to flow right now; it is beaming up as a reflection from the Earth and it is coming down in incandescent rays and a pulse about it. You do know how this energy, the light, stays brighter much longer and how animated it is and magic-like at moments. Well, this is what you are feeling as a result of the speeding up of the planet's energy and it is particularly obvious here because of what you have done just so recently. So, if you may have questions, I am open and happy and any others to whom you might like to speak would also be happy to come in.'

'Mary had some questions and I am going to ask them for her. One of them is what is the energy doing on the property, here at the Isle?'

'Perhaps the best word I could say is it is growing, it is coming up from the ground. As you do know, those angels have been freed, they are allowing their wings to expand; you can almost feel at times the flutter of their wings. There is also an increase from the mountain itself. If you could imagine the mountain being a highly technical centre, much as your own offices and underground workshops are humming and buzzing with ideas with technical innovations – that is coming to you from the mountain. It is not obvious of course, it's not those two towers you see, but it is able to flow over this land, in particular, and is helping to enhance the energy that is already there.

So, you will find a response from the crystals that are under the ground and those strange white-looking rocks that you see – they have gold particles within them, many of them – not all of course – but they are extremely responsive to the type of energy that is being sent in from the mountain, from the spaceships above and also from the opening of the Earth, and there is much that is flowing up and producing a kind of current which is wobbling at the moment. It has not found its place whether it is to be circular, elliptical or whether it be in waves or whether it be just a constant hum over the land – it is settling itself but we will not know for another six months the exact pattern. Does that answer your question my dear?'

'Yes it does, thank you. Another question I have is about the same subject. What could Mary do to help with the energy at the property?'

'I would say remain peaceful and, if you can, admire it and enjoy it. It might be a rainy, cold day and you might say to yourselves: "Well it's not a day to go out and play", but enjoy whatever you can – for example, your day today was beautiful, you enjoyed yourselves, you were out and about looking at the land and admiring it. Enjoy your company, your life where you are and, if you are tired, rest or whatever it is that you can feel freedom through, expressing yourself in art or wanting to take a bicycle ride to the ocean – whatever it is that is liberating for you that is what we are looking for; anything that has to do with expansion, joy, but not to the point where you

77

collapse afterwards. If you were to over-extend yourselves then come back and say: "Oh my, I am really tired – why did I do that?". No, pace yourselves so that you are going gently, flowing with the rhythm of the land.'

'I have a question from Mary about a new property on the Isle – is it in highest wisdom to buy that property?'

'Yes, in fact we are delighted that you have all participated in a forum, if that's the expression you would use, that happened last week and allowed Mary to feel there is freedom from Spirit permitting her to do the kinds of things that we are telling her to do. The property is very much a part of this energy system and it would have been a crying shame if it had not been taken or accepted. We believe you will find an acceptance; you might have to exchange prices for a bit, but it will be yours in a very short amount of time and I think you will enjoy the walks through there and find it quite magical – in some respects more so than here but it will fit in very well to your plan and the work that you do because if you have eight to ten weeks allowed per centre, you see one more centre would give you that many more days to have guests and do your classes.'

'What can that property be used for?'

'Indeed it could be used for visitors, it could be used for people who come in and out. There might be other specialists who want to come to work on an aspect of a type of theory that you are going to develop that will be extremely interesting to people; it might be herbal specialists, my dear, and I look to you when I say that and I think you know why. So, we are waiting for your genius to sprout as well – we are not just speaking of Mary.

So, we will have a herbal conference here and we will also be speaking with psychics of great renown who will choose this spot for a meeting of minds and hearts. You will also deal particularly with people who are coming with a specific kind of dysfunction and you might refer to it as "dyslexia". It will be people who are very much geniuses but cannot express themselves and do not know how to. Some may not even know how to write, my dears, it is that serious – but yet you will recognise their genius. They are not handicapped per se in the sense that they cannot walk or talk. They appear to be very normal people, but their dysfunction has prevented them from having a career or learning to be self reliant even to that extreme; and there will be tears when they come, when they start to unfold and tell you of their drama and what it has done to them. So much will happen and you will probably feel which centre is appropriate, depending upon the particular group that come.

We believe it will not take long before the entire neighbourhood is not only curious but becoming part of the energy system to the point where they will want to be part of what goes on here and ask you if you could not do a class for them. When that happens you will begin to realise the flow is carrying out to more of the Isle and it will encompass much of what goes on in the entire Isle, but that will take two years before you have them all coming to eat out of your hands, so to speak.'

'I would like some guidance.'

'Again my dear, the rest. I cannot say more to you for the process is starting, you are being prepared, this is a very, very large transition for you. Everything cannot happen at once and we need to prepare you for there is not much time. We are getting very close to that deadline and we would like you to be ready in your body at least two days before the 1st of August so that when it will happen you will be at peace and there will not be a major issue – that is why this instability within you is even being accelerated right now so that it will happen now and we can deal with it. So when you are on that other level and you are going through changes fast, rapidly, you cannot have your system blowing up or bleeding or your thyroid going off. Do you see, it is very critical for us right now to

79

have access – especially to your brain – because that is controlling all of the areas in your body that we do not have to touch directly.'

'I have one more question about something you said earlier – you said that the energy would take about six months to settle down here. Is it a good idea to do a couple of classes or not?'

'Excellent, that would enhance the energy. Do you see, it is being used for its purpose and it is not a property that is meant to just sit and be idle. It is fed with the idea that people are coming here to learn more about themselves and who they are. That will start a small circle of people who will go home and speak about it. It will go much faster along with the news than you had expected and this is what the Isle does and does very well in a positive sense. So, we would like you to feed the positive aspects and not the negative ones.'

'Thank you.'

'We would like to see you grow with this energy and also find yourself in a calmer space so that you can bring in what we are sending to you as we are trying right now. You are too tired to integrate it and we do not want to go in and upset the balance right now so we are waiting for you to find that balance of peace and harmony. When it is there then we will start working on you and you will begin your process much as Mary is going through, which will mean periods of pain, of perhaps aches, bodily disruptions that you don't always under-stand, but these other two can be here to help you and allow you to go through it.'

'What am I going to go through?'

'Would someone else like to answer!?'

'I would say experiencing a closer relationship with the God

Source, knowing that certain Guides are present to assist in the opening.'

'I could say in three weeks it could start. If you will allow yourself to be available and to open yourself through meditation, prayer, great gratitude and just to be one with us. We are not coming here so as to present a dogma or to say: "It must be this way". What we enjoy is the collaboration whereby you look for us and that we are welcomed and we are not bringing this as a punishment though many have accused us of this.

No one in this room has thought of that, but we do hear that ascension is nothing but pain and why are we being told to go through this when nothing is happening. There are threats, there are rather violent remarks and many have even dropped from their spiritual path because they did not like the pain. Now we make it available to you to choose; of course, there is always that choice, but you will find my dear you keep going and I believe you have that kind of make up. You will discover a kind of commitment, to keep going no matter what. It does not mean that if your body is really aching and there is nothing you can do about it, then of course you do cancel your appointments. That is what we would recommend, but if you are finding that once you've had breakfast, you are feeling better and you are able to function – perhaps for half a day – then you would go to the office and then come home early. You have to arrange yourself to fit in to how you are feeling which does allow you to be connected to your body and to know it well. Sometimes the signs are there that you go nowhere and you may have to cancel a holiday or a departure or whatever, but it is Spirit speaking through you, my dear, and it is a gift.'

'I hope that this time frame here will let me sort it out because I'm feeling really tired.'

'By all means, my dear, and do let your emotions out. You have been so brave and courageous and carried on despite all odds and made a wonderful path for Mary that she could not have accomplished without your help, my dear. Your intuition, your strength, your perseverance and your courage – do you realise who you are? Some day we will do a session together to make you more aware of the beauty of your soul and how it is trying to connect with you so that your lower self is rising up to connect with that Higher Self, so that when you will carry on your work there will be an amalgam, a blending of those two energies and can you see the Goddess emerging, beautiful white robed, splendid in all of her assurance and beauty? What an image for women to look to. We are counting on you my dear. There is much that you have to do and much that we want you to be aware of and available for as that energy comes through. You will see the changes in others, you will see and witness what happens to Mary and then you will say: "What about myself?" – you are next. So, as you let yourself go and allow those emotions free reign it means that you may scream – that is allowed – you may shout, you may sing, you may run out, you may do whatever is allowed, what you allow yourself to do. Do not hesitate, know those emotions. The only thing holding you back right now is your inability to feel free enough to express them. You are in a loving environment and you can have all the support that you need for this. We want you to be freer my dear. When you are tired you know it and you can announce it to your comrades and say: "I am sorry, I must go right now", with no explanation and go home and rest, play with your dog, be whatever you want to be. Other questions dear ones?'

'I think I would like just to say about your Spirit Guides. I would like you to meditate. This is Archangel Michael speaking, my dear, so you may say: "I am not sure who my Guide is", and I will say at the moment if you could look to Master Hilarian – he comes as a healer, he was St Paul in the Bible and he has very much the energy that you are part of and that he can assist you with. So, if you would just sit in the morning, early, and receive his message for the day and find a great deal of comfort in it to the point where you can commune with him and ask questions and receive answers.'

'Many of the light workers are moving on and are disappearing from this Earth but it is not from giving up or relapsing into self pity that they are doing it – they are asking Spirit to guide them and accepting whatever Spirit brings to them, much as you are doing my dears, but we have chosen for you to be on this Earth solid, real, visible at the same time. You are going to work in the spheres unknown yet to yourselves in your conscious memory, but soon to become part of your lives, so expanded, so magical and mystical that you will wonder how did you ever survive on this Earth previously. In fact, we enjoy those moments thinking of how you are now and how you shall be in a few months' time.'

BECOMING FISHERS OF MEN

Archangel Raphael

'I am Raphael. Greetings. You will find me a bit different from the others. Know that it is a joy for me to be in an earthly body and to witness the sight. Do you remember when the nets were put out when Jesus was on board ship and the fish came in? Is this not a marvel, a manifestation in truth? You are the "fishers" of men and women. Do you see your role? It is being emphasised by these fish and you will be there to feed them, you will be able to create the right energy for them, baskets in which to break the fish and the bread into many pieces and feed the multitude – not always with food may I say – but with your spiritual teachings, with the words of Grace and Love that you will inspire people with; and you will know the right thing to say to each one.

It would be a happy day when more can come, but until the multitudes may be welcomed here, you, too, must be solid in what is truth and what is not truth. Do you see, your hearts are so open, you are such beautiful souls. You do not see the mischievousness and the scheming and the plotting and what's going on behind doors. You feel it instinctively – I am very aware of that, but it's not always in time to be able to say: "No, I do not want this", and to reject it.

You and Mary need to practice exercises together whereby you will say something very outrageous to Mary and she will respond: "I'm sorry, I find that rude and out of order". You will say all the things you have never dared say to one another, but you will make it a game and provoke each other and say: "I am not satisfied with this report – I would like to have something definite on my desk by tomorrow morning", then you will respond: "I am not getting the instructions I need and I am not able to do the work because I don't find that I am being looked after here". Whatever it is you wish to do, do it with laughter and pleasantries. You will enjoy one another and learn to simply say "no". Then someone will ask you for something and you will say "no". Now, to anyone who does not know the game you might have a twinkle in your eye or a wink, but to Mary you can say "no". You can punch your fist on the desk and say: "I don't want to, it's not convenient at this time and what you are asking is totally unacceptable", and I need to say to you this: It is in jest and in laughter – but I am very serious that you have been so kindly, so good to so many that saying "no" is not a part of your vocabulary and it is all to your credit. If you are on our side, we would welcome you with open arms, we would give you a better set of wings than you already have. We would put labels on you – "Chief Angel Overseer of Bad People" – and we would welcome you and sing hymns to you of joy. It is, unfortunately, a devious and dark world you are living upon. I believe as Mary will unearth some of her books, she may give them to you. We are part of the Guides who have been with her, as well, have helped write this book saying how the negativity is increasing. As you know, you are approaching rapidly the photon belt. You will learn how your entire solar system is moving into the shape of a quarter moon. As it bumps into it, there is resistance and you could almost see sparks coming from this interaction. It shall be dangerous – your Earth shall be on fire. In certain spots, it will be erupting, there will be tidal waves, water will be overflowing, other places will have droughts, oceans will dry up, seas – like the Dead Sea – will go dry, and there will be much misery and crying which will break your hearts. I have to say ours, as well. Many have been warned and know that there is – not impending doom – but a time when they know they must make their choice whether or not to be one with Spirit and this time is coming my dear. What Mary is seeing in all of her confusion and all of the trials and tribulations that are going on with the players she has chosen is that she is finding, to her dismay, they are not one with Spirit. If there is not clarity around her and her businesses, there will not be prosperity, there will not be the abundance created among you so that you can reach out gladly and help this one and manifest food and manifest shelter for those who are homeless. You shall be able to do it as will Mary. She will have her first example today of manifestation. You may remark the results. You will say: "Oh this is curious – so and so phoned and said they are not available to work with you or to come to the meetings that have been scheduled", and it will happen around you as a result of this prayer: "Asking that those who are involved with negative energy do not come near these projects". And it shall be fulfilled, for this is a gift being given to both of you and you have earned it well my dear.'

'Thank you.'

'Well done and you will find as you do meditate and you see things happening around you that are unjust, that people who are unkindly continue to do what they have done and go on being unpunished and it shall not happen around you nor to those you choose to be with who are truly one with Spirit. It's a time now that the only thing that matters is Spirit and you shall see yourselves – you and Mary – you will evolve as angels, true angels that you are, and you shall become transparent. You shall see one another but the others will not see you. You may even hold hands and walk out of a crowded hall and no one will notice you. You shall have great fun doing so for it is very close at hand. We were urging Mary on last night in her dreams, to understand that what she believed was pure and innocent is not. You will touch people in a way where you will just be talking and, as you are talking, you will send people energy and love without even knowing it; it's so natural for you. They just feel happy around you.'

86

'I hope they all turn out to be better human beings and that we could help open them to their true beingness.'

'And you are doing that. It is very comforting.'

'I feel very good, thank you.'

'And I pray that you will always feel good and you may take that affirmation that Mary has taken and was given by Archangel Michael in saying that: "I am one with Spirit and the Holy Father and I am being taken care of". We do not ask you to be irresponsible, but we know at this point who you are and where your longings are to serve others and because your hearts are pure and because you come asking for others and very little for yourselves, you do need support now. You need to know that inasmuch as you are strong and you are powerful in the sense of Spirit, of holding Archangel Michael's sword when it is fitting and being one with St George and slaying the dragons that you see around you, you may do it and you may make this manifestation part of your vocabulary. You may even come alone in the beginning, yet we would like you and Mary to be together, for it is comforting to know that you are both here, kneeling if possible, before the cross – much as Sananda has done and so has Kuthumi. They know that cross well.

As you kneel and you attune yourselves to Spirit, you will feel a surging within you of love, of tremendous Love and Light surrounding you. If at that moment you were to reach out and touch someone, they would be healed instantly – such is your power in manifesting, but we do not ask you to use it for that. Check with one another, check with us as to what you would like to manifest, how you would like to do it, is it highest wisdom, is it working for the highest good of all human kind or for a select élite who know full well that a prayer is being made and they will not know. So, you will seal the door please – if you wish to close it, you may do so. It would be a time for you both to be kneeling before the cross and to say the prayer that you have written on your papers.

87

You do not need to do it now. Think very clearly about what is your message that you are bringing and make sure that it does not bring somebody into bondage with something that they might not choose as a soul. Look at it from the higher perspective of what the soul would be wanting for this entity and the soul wants light to come in, wants to see this being expanded and to become part of the ascension process. So, you would see an opportunity for someone to be out there reaching out to many beings, to be able to assist them, to help, to be able to expand in his or her energy by asking you questions – how may I best do this, how may I be at peace when I go home and my wife and children are asking me things? How do you do it?'

'We would ask them to speak of their pain and their problems; to cry or shout if needs be.'

'There it is, you are not creating a constriction or a boundary or a taboo. You are just there for them.'

'That's the best part of it.'

'And that's what people do not know how to do.'

'That's very unfortunate.'

'Most unfortunate, my dear. And what I ask only of you both is to constantly keep in touch with Spirit, with the Supreme Universal power – I believe Mary explained that to you. It is not that it is the only way to address the Holy Father – certainly in your private prayers you may use Holy Father, whatever you are familiar with, like Mother Mary. For this particular exercise it is warranted to ask the Supreme Universal Power to manifest the force. It is the force that will act through you and as I say it, the power is coming into this chapel. So, perhaps, let us close now. You might be well advised to·close the door and you could both sit on that bench perhaps opposite the cross and when it comes time to make your request for the negativity to disappear or to disperse as Mary wanted to see "it" happen, you could both say the prayer together and that would make it more powerful. Blessings and love upon you and know that this is a gift that is coming to you from your Supreme Universal Power, the Holy of Holy, the great and awesome one who has seen in you a fit vessel to whom he can confide in and can trust that your children are his children and that your wishes are his wishes. Go in peace my loved ones and know that you are very, very blessed and honoured and I am, as well, in your presence.'

'Thank you.'

* * *

'Good morning Mary. This is a beautiful Sunday morning in your chapel. I am Archangel Gabriel and I come to you once again at a critical time in your evolution. It is not the only time I have been present; there are so many lifetimes, Mary. We shall sit and laugh, perhaps around a fire, drinking hot tea, enjoying the company, enjoying the lightness and the life that has brought us together in so many lifetimes. You do not know it, my dear, but many times I have envied your ability to go out and interact with toughness, with lies, with rugged people who do not know Light and Love and honesty and you have been there as a soldier. Sometimes I wanted to put a helmet on you and arm you with an armoured suit and say to you: "It's all right, Mary, we are behind you". You must have known it though for you carried on despite the odds that seemed to be against you. Yes, you were burned at the stake. Yes, you had your head rolled off and guillotined. Yes, you were tied down and tortured. Many were the ways that they sought to destroy you – "they" being those who wanted to control you, afraid and suspicious of what your powers were. Never have your powers been so strong nor so clear nor so ready to be set in action and, as I speak, I look out upon those beautiful clear, sparkling blue waters and I reflect upon how wondrous this world is; the calm of the ocean, the reflection of light that it carries, the fish that swim under the surface quite oblivious to what is going on above are all part of God's realm; his creatures, his reflecting power and as he may shine it upon a sparkling stone, a diamond – look how it reflects out to so many, to so much. That, my dear, is what you are about to do. You need your training though, Mary, and we acknowledge that you are tired. You have worked now for well on to sixty-three years and I do say you have not lost your time, so what may have appeared to surge as a loss of time was gaining experience, Mary. You could not read this in a book, nor could you hear about it from us or from others, for your experiences are yours. Would you exchange those memories of Sananda, even at the moment of his torture? Would you ask to be removed from that gift that was given to you back then, knowing full well now the consequences and how the suffering came to you amidst the joy, the pride and the honour? There are so many facets to these experiences – what may appear to be the worst are not the worst and they may be your best ones, for those are the ones that you will cherish and remember – either not to do again or to hold on to – to believe that you may trust that there are wondrous beings around you who do wish to grow spiritually and who will be your honoured and most respected disciples. You will come back shortly Mary – within five months – and your time away will not be lost. You will be honoured, you will be resting, laughing, alive as you have never known before, watching your body be restructured – the new one – watching and admiring the souls around you who have dedicated their lives to uplifting this planet, into, not just the fifth dimension, but other ones. Far, far away they come and they are impressed by souls such as you, and I must say it is a gift you have given me to allow me to be there for you at this time. Yes, you recognised the Arcturians last night – they are the most diligent of all those beings coming from out of space and they love the beings who are evolving towards Spirit and have known you and recognised you since you were a baby. That is why they have allowed and witnessed the transfer that is happening – we will not mention it but you know what I am referring to. Now, I say to you to prepare yourself – there is no preparation – you merely carry on with your tasks and have yourself ready for tomorrow morning – a handbag prepared, your shoes, your clothes and certainly your attaché case and then you shall go to bed and give up to Spirit that which belongs to Spirit. There is to be no worry, Mary. There is nothing that you need to do that you have not done. There is no one you need to write to nor do you need to connect with anyone – they are the ones who owe you a service. And, if you are not there Monday morning to take that important telephone call from New York then you know that your replacement shall be there, shall be eloquent and shall be convincing and knowing that this is where help will be coming from. Do not worry about any kind of confrontation – it shall not happen, Mary. You have put out your prayer and have asked that it be manifest, that the negativity around you be removed and that is happening. Do you trust, my dear, fully? If this is the last gesture you make upon this globe for the moment, it would be a memorable one. Trust has long been an issue with you for you have had reason not to trust, but when you trust in Spirit you know you shall never be betrayed and that is my bond with you, to see to it that you are never betrayed. Dear Mary, I weep with that which you have suffered and I know that it has been trying and you have felt so abandoned and we watched, observing, not able to intervene because it was not the order that was given to us, and when we were told: "Now archangels, you may come to Mary", we crowded at the doorway saying: "But we want to be first", and laughingly you knew it and you dealt with all of us; chiding us in your sleeping hours and being playful and as loving as you are always when you are in our sphere. Do not be worried that you have been too gentle with many of these souls – they would not have understood if you had been severe and calling out to them with reproaches – that is not your way. Some day they shall come to understand it. Put down the veil, Mary, hold it in front of you – it is a shimmering one and you shall not be observed, for your eyes are like mirrors and they will reflect but they do also attract, so try not to bring in anything that does not belong to you and that you do not need. Remember

91

my dear, recite your prayer as you did last night – any of your favourite prayers – and if the pain becomes intense, ask once again if please you may move or get up and circulate, then go back to bed. Trust that after midnight it shall become concrete and perhaps by bedtime you will be tired and have slept. So the transition may happen without your memory but at any rate I, Archangel Gabriel, reassure you my dear and loving Mary that it shall happen this night or tomorrow morning early and you shall be welcomed as you have never been welcomed anywhere on this planet Earth. We love you – all of us – and we welcome and rejoice the moment that we shall be together, laughing as you so love to do and chiding one another cheerfully and looking to the future to see that wondrous path. The veil is being lifted Mary and you shall see it all, you shall know where you will go, when you will go, with whom you shall travel and how it will manifest. Your work shall be glorious and we bid you adieu for now, asking you to rest this day. Leave your worries on the doorstep and proceed through that doorjamb filled with light and promise and happiness with no fear, with nothing other than your love to accompany you. All shall be taken care of as only God knows how to do. My love to you Mary and may you have a blessed and most fulfilling Sunday. Adieu my dear.'

BEING BRIGHTER AND LIGHTER
EACH DAY

Kuthumi

'Are you Kuthumi?'

'Yes dear one.'

'Is there anything you would like to say for my associate?'

'For you, dear one, I have seen you go through a lot of turmoil, conflict, betrayal, as if put in a washer, in a blender and still you are together and since you have been going through all this, you are still together and holding that wonderful energy. Be there and be proud for what you have been doing and what you are about to receive and it is by dealing with matters like this, that this brings out the best in you.

No matter what, you are cheerful. So, dear one, go strongly and don't let any of those little bugs try to steal the wonderful light and the love that you have in you. I pray that you shall light up stronger and brighter every day. It is just like looking at the Sun in a beautiful clear morning coming out of the horizon and that wonderful Sun is not just there for this little island, for the United States, Europe, but for the whole world it shines; yet even in this world of yours there are still a lot of dark places; there are places that do not want to see the Sun, they are trying to block it off. The light that you are bringing is the light that eventually even those who have their eyes closed

93

will see and feel. Yes, feel the warmth that you are bringing towards them. So please, dear one, don't let little things like this try and take that energy from you. If you breathe in and relax and feel the energy that is around you, you will grow stronger and stronger and you will win any battles that come your way.'

'Thank you Kuthumi. One last thing – I worked on my associate last night and, as you know, I hadn't healed for a long time. It was a beautiful experience. I could hear the Medical Assistant Professionals talking. It was almost as if they were sharing their thoughts with me and there was such a wonderful feeling in doing that work. I can see now the progress that has been made and measure it by that lovely experience.'

'Indeed. You had the patience, you waited and now you see the beauty and there is more to come, so do have fun and enjoy yourself and don't let any turmoil come between you and the things that you love to do. So, I shall go now and leave you both in peace and by all means, wherever you are – walking along the street, by the pool, in your office or anybody's office – ask for us or think of us and we will be there to support you and guide you whenever you need us. Amen.'

CALLING ON ONE'S HIGHER SELF

St Francis

'I am Kuthumi, as you know, dear Mary, and your friend knows me as St Francis.'

'Do you prefer to be called one or the other Kuthumi?'

'Either way – whichever you feel most comfortable with.'

'Thank you for coming.'

'I just want to enjoy your energy and bask in it, but we do have much to ask you this morning. Is it all right to ask our questions?'

'Yes dear one.'

'I have a stone here, in this chapel, and it's over by the candles. It supposedly has a message for me. Is there a particular place I need to put it until I find the key?'

'At this chapel, it would be beautiful to leave it here until you find a key for it, that way it will not be lost and it will be blessed with the wonderful energy that you all surround it with and give to it.'

'Is it to be used here on the island?'

'Not at this particular time, no.'

'Thank you Kuthumi. I wanted to go and talk to our friends this morning in the portal and is it appropriate to ask them to help me with my desire to channel music?'

'They would be glad to, yes.'

'Are there times at which I need to speak to them?'

'They will advise you on that and they will like your presence, dear, very much.'

'Wonderful, I shall be there this morning if that's in divine order. I want to thank you Kuthumi. Is there anyone in particular I need to call on in my business meetings, for example, my Higher Self?'

'Your Higher Self will be the greatest one to have there with you and even if you can call an angel to be present there on either side of the table, but at the same time concentrate on your Higher Self and have it there to protect you but have an angel just to observe what is going on either side of the table just in case any of them try to misjudge you. They will get them in line.'

'Would it be fitting that I smudge the room before we have the meeting?'

'It's not necessary, but have one of your favourite crystals with you.'

'Thank you Kuthumi. I'm just very angry deep down and I am sorry.'

'I quite understand, that's why I ask you to use your gut feelings but hold your love at the same time – don't explode.'

'Is there any message for my friend, Kuthumi?'

'Just ask him not to worry so much. He's like you in many ways: pressure comes up and he takes it on himself. Just tell him to let the Guides take care of it and to light up and let him glow again and then the problems will disappear underneath his feet as he walks lightly with the Holy Father on one hand and our guidance on the other and no one will ever bring him down.'

'Will the Kryon Group inform us of what we are to do to be more perfectly aligned to this new grid system?'

'They will guide you through that way.'

'So I may go out there now and perhaps talk to them?'

'By all means – they are waiting.'

'Thank you Kuthumi. My heart is wanting to say it embraces all that you are representing and all the help you are bringing to us.'

'Dear one, you take this love that you receive and carry it for the rest of the day and may your wonderful meetings be delightful and full of joy and let no harm come to you. May God keep you and look out for you so that you will come out shining on this wonderful day that we call Tuesday.'

USING MUSIC TO FEEL AT PEACE

St Francis

'Finally, you both made it. We have been waiting for you. As you probably know, I am St Francis and you are always welcome to a wonderful place that is blessed as this one is. Yes, dear one?'

'Thank you St Francis. I have to thank you for coming to me in the American south when we were visiting a friend and his wife. I was wondering if you have anything to say to me about that: whether we are going to work there or are we to open vortices there? Do you want us to use the Betar machines in our centres? Could you give me some kind of help in that respect?'

'Yes there will be some work done there but not yet. We are looking at about nine to twelve months' time. Yes, it will be a very, very honourable place for you to work and the dear ones you bring together, indeed, but don't rush it. You have so much to accomplish in these few months ahead of you so just let it be and take one step at a time. Spirit has its ways of working and when the right property comes up, you will see it. Yes, at the time put out your interest in it and you can review it for a later date.'

'Thank you. I enjoyed being with my friend and his wife

and I am wondering are we to use those Betar machines in the work that we will be doing?'

'That will be good to do because that will help balance people. They do need to have faith and any kind of movement of energy that brings them at peace is a challenge for them to go further. That is just one of the examples to some of those that don't have faith: put them in there and see how they feel with the music that they choose to listen to. It will automatically become like a trance and they will feel very, very at ease.'

'Beautiful. Would it help someone who is an alcoholic and a drug addict?'

'It will help those who are willing to go for that first step and seek help. They may joke about it but, when they come out of it, they will say: "Well this stupid thing really works!", but often they will not go alone, so, please try to invite them there with a friend.'

'Oh, that's so precious. Thank you. I just believe that many can be helped and I thank you for your support and advice. Also, is there one vortex to be opened or several? Do we open all the vortices or one or two at a time?'

'Dear one, that is one of my favourite subjects. Yes, you will find a property that you will purchase with one in it and a few little ones around. Go through it and you will open just one but once you open that major one, it will activate the others around it because one centre is like the Sun. Look what it lights up around it and magnifies; an incredible force. It makes everything look nice and bright whereas in the dark, everything looks dull and at the moment, those vortices are in the dark but if you open one there, that will be the Sun shining on the rest of them and they will become reality.'

'Would you suggest that I find a crystal, if possible an earth-keeper, to put on that vortex?'

99

'In the one that you are going to find on your property, yes. It is always good to keep that as a balance and once you activate it with a crystal on it, that automatically sends signals to others and, for example, even if you open a vortex, it is like a beautiful flower shining and opening. It is like a very bright sun and once you put the crystal on top of it, it reflects light back to the others on the ground. Would you like me to explain that a little bit better for you?'

'Yes, I would.'

'Okay. You have your flower facing up with all its beautiful points and then once you put the crystal on top of it, it automatically shoots through the ground onto the other vortices around it. This one will take it up – as you open a flower or plant a tree – it just comes up and once you put the crystal on top of it, everything just starts to shoot to different areas, to activate the other vortices around it.'

'I see it almost as firecrackers, once you start to light one or two on the 4th of July then they go off in succession.'

'Great. As you can see, your third eye is getting better and better.'

'Thank you. And the date: I will know it, will I?'

'Yes indeed.'

'Thank you. Well, speaking of vortices, I thought the Isle was rich in vortices until I went to the American south. Is it still necessary that I go there?'

'No, you don't have to go there for that purpose. If you go to this other vortex, all your vortices will be communicating together and once you activate this one here, you will see the results all around the others. I would like to see a few of you meditate on this and visualise these peace-keepers sending signals, like you have just finished saying to one another; a group of three or four would be great and just align them. In other words, guide them to their extra point even if you have to draw lines on a map and just visualise this wonderful communication together. You have activated quite a few of them. Make them all work together now. Connect one with the other and you should see magnificent and wonderful things happen.'

'So that would be our vortices around the world?'

'Yes. You put them all in place and you just line them up and any time you are prepared to work together, as I have mentioned, with three or four, you can bring all these wonderful energies together and it's just like saying: "I have found my sister, I have found my brother and we all connect together now; we all live as one". The strength will be wonderful and the love that every human being will feel from this wonderful energy will be a miracle thanks to all the wonderful work that all of you have done and have put your minds to. I know you can accomplish this mission.'

'Thank you St Francis. Is there a time when we need to do it?'

'I am not here to give you a time. It is whenever it is convenient to you dear ones. They have been waiting all this time, they can wait a little bit longer, but it is up to you.'

'Thank you. I treasure everything you say and pray that we will do it according to the "Divine Will".'

'Thank you.'

'May I just ask a question about a friend in the Isle? She lost her husband recently and seems very sad and lost herself. Is there anything I could tell her that might encourage her and lift up her heart?'

'Yes; do comfort her. Tell her even that it is a great loss to her to lose a wonderful human being like him, but think on the bright side. He is already in that other dimension and he could be there with her at any time she wishes, but do not hang on emotionally. See him as he would have always been because, dear ones, the wonderful angels are all around human kind and if you just call upon their names, they will be there for them but, at the same time, do not get too attached to them. I would hate to see her have this high hope in her and feel like he is still there as a human; no, but he is still present and just tell her that the worst is over for him. Now he is in the wonderful world that we are all to be part of one day. If she just puts her love in God, the Divine One, to fill that emptiness on her side and ask if he can be present there whenever she needs a warm welcome from anyone.'

'Thank you. That's beautiful St Francis. I have a personal question to ask about my healing work. It seems like I have moments of contraction and almost like energy pulsing through me in uneven streaks. Is there anything I am doing to block it or is it just natural for right now?'

'It's not the blockage and what you are feeling now is your energy with the spiritual energy coming through you and as that energy comes through you and you send it to the client and he/she becomes hot-warm, hot-warm-cold and you feel that. As you have been bringing in this energy and doing this healing for a while now, the more you do it, the more energy will come in through you. Just let it float right through you because at the moment, you still feel that insecure sort of way when you are not sure of things like this. You tend to tighten your muscles and hold on to what comes in. By doing this you almost reject the healing energy. You must let it flow through your body and just be as calm as possible. You are doing a great job, congratulations and just let it go through. You will feel great and thank the Holy Ones for being there for you because it is an honour for them to come down and heal others through your flesh.'

102

'I have only one more question St Francis. Could you tell me if there is anything further I need to do to facilitate the transition that I am going through?'

'The pain, the agony that humans receive I feel is unfair but, then again, who am I to judge the humans. I suggest that every time you receive pain or negative energy, send up your highest souls to the High Divine One and see it, that wonderful light, coming down through your crown chakra. Know that as it comes down, it cleans your body. You can do that in the mornings when you wake up or, indeed, every time you feel that you have been worked upon, but ask for guidance first: "Is it all right for me to do this?", and they will respond, "Yes". If you are in pain or in such an uncomfortable way that you would like to be more comfortable then they will help you. No one should be suffering and if you just ask for the Holy One to come down and say: "Yes, I am going through this change but please what can I do to make it easier on my behalf? Am I allowed to use the Golden, White Light for this healing?" And you will receive whatever you ask for but you must ask, please, dear one, and you shall not suffer.'

'Thank you St Francis. Do I ask for my Higher Self to come down or just any entity, any Ascended Master?'

'Any of the Ascended Masters will do but you can ask for the highest one of all – our Holy Father – and just let that wonderful energy restore you, and He will come down and help you, dear one. After all you are his temple and he will be honoured to come down and help you. He doesn't want to see any humans that He created, that are his loving children, suffer in this world.'

'Thank you St Francis. I have no more questions. Bless you.'

'I will pray with you at all times; that you wake up shining,

103

singing and happy with no more pain and that you will always be one of the most blessed masters of the universe. My dear one, goodbye and may our Holy Father bless you.'

'Goodbye.'

ON HEALING CHILDREN

Mother Mary

'I am Mother Mary and I will be talking about the children. I will come down and give all the knowledge that I have on this subject for both of you and those wonderful little light beings that need your guidance at all times.'

'Could you tell us when Mother Mary?'

'To heal the children the sooner the better, but you dear one are not ready for that yet. April, Easter time: that will be a great time in memories. There is so much they will bring to our hearts and that will be a good time for you to heal those wounded little hearts.'

'How will I be accepted by the parents and the people at large?'

'You will be loved by them; you will know your way around at the time. That time will be a good time for you to do that particular work and you will be amazed at the questions that are going to come towards you and you will answer them.'

'Mother Mary, is that a time to start working on older patients as well?'

'You will have your hands full with the younger children first and then move one step further after your work is completed with them, but first you are to heal those little ones. Don't get yourself too involved – one step at a time. You will get around to it.'

'It always makes me sad to think of the little ones that are suffering. Thank you.'

'Dear one, be happy. Look what you are going through. It hurts me to see you bleeding on the inside. Open up and be joyful. It's an honour to be here with all of you so please, I beg you, be happy and enjoy the moments to come because those children are going to look up to you and say thanks for your gift of love and your healing.'

'Could you tell me what age I will work on – up to fifteen?'

'You can start as soon as they are born; right up to fourteen. I'm looking at thirteen, fourteen – yes.'

'Beautiful, thank you. I wanted to ask, as part of the ascension which my friend and I are both going through, if it would be advisable for us to visualise our light bodies carrying us upwards through the clouds and ask Archangel Michael to sever the cords that are connecting us to Earth?'
'That is wonderful. It is good to visualise that which you will be able to see all around you. It's just like a 180-degree turn: you just turn and you see everything around you. You will be able to see where you are going, what you left behind and what's ahead of you. Yes, do practice that. You are almost there actually. I can see you pulling your wings out and trying to cut this dragging cord with your will, but, dear one, ask for his guidance and he will be glad to help you and lift you up.'

'You mean Archangel Michael?'

'Yes, indeed.'

'Thank you. And my friend as well?'

'Yes. He can start practising but he still has a little way to go. It will be a good example for him and once he has a look at you, he will try extra hard believe me.'

'Will I be closer to you in doing this work with the light bodies?'

'You already are in many ways and it is an honour to work with you and welcome you back.'

'Thank you Mother Mary. The big question is how do we work on people who do not ask for our help? Yesterday I saw this young lady with cancer, a young twelve-year-old girl with cancer in her throat and I knew I could help her but I didn't know how to reach out to someone who doesn't ask for me?'

'This way, as I say again, you will be able to reach out until your astral light body, your energy will go through these human beings. Picture and visualise them in front of you, bring them to the light and ask your beautiful Guardian Angels around you just to focus on working with her. You don't have to be present as long as you bring her to you, just visualise he or she, bring that person to you and work in their belief system, in their spiritual system – not where the pain is, not where the disease is at the moment – just bring them in closer and once you bring them in and that Spirit inside or closer to you, send them the meanings of God's message: "Dear one, if there is no help for you in the world of medicine, God still loves you and he is in the process of healing you, and they will come to you", but you must focus on that person and tell them there is a cure and you will be glad to do it if they will be willing to accept it. They will accept, dear one, because it will be your Spirit talking to his or her Spirit and they communicate a lot easier than human beings. Once you can get that connection, the Spirit will accept the work that you are doing and then eventually this human being will be healed thanks to your wonderful work with Spirit and the Angelic Kingdom.'

'I have only one last question, Mother Mary. I know my friend is a healer and we didn't know how to start working on his ability: could you give me some instruction in that respect?'

'You do have some good books on this and, for example, he can use one of these channels as a guinea pig without them even knowing what kind of work he is doing. They will know spiritually but let them work on different movements. If you can, bring the energy to the feet, to the arms and let the children participate. They understand far more than adults want to believe. Ask them where it hurts and if they can talk to it, and make them move that energy towards that toothache or wherever it is that hurts them and he will practice this. When he has this technique he will be able to practice on outsiders. Have faith and he will do a great job.'

'You have blessed us beyond belief Mother Mary.'

'Thanks for all the wonderful questions that you asked. It is always an honour to be here and to guide you in the right direction. I may bless you all with all my heart and I will help you unfold all the wonderful things in your life.'

* * *

'This is Skakus and I tend to forget my volume control so you might have to tell me it's time to regulate the speed and the force with which I send my message through. Now I am very happy to be here because I do find a bit of turmoil this morning, and if I can be of any help? You know that your angels and all those guardians and the keepers of God's peace are with you and will never, ever let you down so do not think that there is a moment they have abandoned you or forgotten you or given you the wrong angel or confused you in any way.

108

We can only say all of us on our side applaud your being here so regularly. Early mornings seem very good times when it is peaceful here on the island and, if it works for you, we are more than delighted to find you here. So what can I do for you today?'

'What can be done to help Mary sleep better?'

'It is good from time to time to call on the angels and Celestial Healers, and it certainly does bring about a major cleansing, but it is not in the long run the way to avoid having these negative energies impact her body. She must do more work with the Light that is above her. Now, of course, if there are too many negative energies within her system, she cannot reach up and find the Light, but sometimes it is too easy to clean up and then negative energies find a clean room, so to speak, and they come rushing in again finding it very wonderful that someone has cleaned up for them. Well I would suggest at this time she work more closely with St Germain and the Violet Flame, asking him please to provide a very special Violet Flame that would protect her at all times when going into a building, when driving in to town, when coming home in the afternoon; that's something she could use on a regular basis. It seems the shield overhead has not done the work that has been anticipated because Mary has a particular frailty and it is an opening that unfortunately these mis-chievous beings can perceive and they find their way in despite the work that she has been doing to put her shield up.

So, we would suggest working with St Germain, also with Mother Mary, in the sense that she would ask for her cloak of Golden Light to come down and turn it into almost a cape whereby it would be a cape with a hood; the kind that Little Red Riding Hood had and if she could put this golden cloak around her and over her head, using the Violet Flame from St Germain, this would combine the work with St Germain, bringing in the Violet Flame and that would enhance the purple which is around her and as she brings down the cloak from

109

Mother Mary then the purple lining would naturally be on the inside and, as she covers herself in that purple lining, she will grow more accustomed to wearing the golden mantle. It will be very soothing for her and almost something she can touch at this time. So, I would recommend this technique because she has tried many different ways and you have suggested things and it has not always worked, so we have had to come in and do excess zealousness in order to repair that which has been damaged and this must not go on because there is no tranquillity for this soul. She needs to rest at night and not have to worry about headaches and voyagers inside her.'

'Thank you.'

'Have you any questions?'

'One more. Is the big earth-keeper the right piece for the Isle and what will it do?'

'Indeed and I am glad you asked because to bring such a heavy piece in and have it distort the energy would be very disastrous for all of us on all levels. We do need to have you check specifically when it comes to crystals. I know Mary was very upset yesterday when she thought one of those meteorites had been lost and that it was affecting your big crystal; fortunately it was not the case but please check in with the crystal regularly to see if it is content with its spin, with the balance that is around it, whether there is a force pulling it off centre and if there is anything you could do to help now and then. You might just stand there and hold the energy while the sun is out and welcome it to come down and bathe the crystal sending it Light and encouragement for, in truth, this crystal is probably doing more work than any of the other crystals that you have put in place. The new earth-keeper that you will bring over to the Isle will be much as a bath tub. Now this seems strange for a crystal to look like a container – they usually do the opposite – but this particular one is going to enclose different types of energy within it.'

'Could you explain to us why it has such a strange shape?'

'Well, this is a crystal in the shape of a flower so when those energies come in and impact the crystal and go down through it they are already worked upon and they are stronger and more vibrant and, also, will reflect energy out. So, you are getting energy going into the Earth and moving about on all that northern part of the globe and above you are having a very incredible type of reflection of what is going on below, but it is more of a soothing screen-like effect so that when radical changes tend to hit the Isle, it will absorb it. If you could imagine cotton wool suddenly coming out of the wonderful mouthpiece of that vortex and the cotton wool absorbing all of the extremes, the sharp edges, the ways that people would tend to erupt and deposit all those bad energies, such as anger and whatever. It will soothe things. It will also soothe the winds as they come across those plains; it will contain the softness within the area and, as it expands, it becomes more encouraged and enlivened by the energy in that area; it will extend out beyond the Isle and will go very far. I will not say it will go as far as the North Pole but certainly as far up as the Hebrides: it will cover the totality of Ireland, Scotland and England and start to move down to the continent. This will be extremely powerful.

It will take about another two years before it is fully felt outside the Isle but within the Isle in six months' time, you will see a noticeable difference.'

'Thank you. This information is extremely valuable.'

'Thank you and I bless you and pray that the love and light of the Holy Spirit be with you, to guide you, to surround you and to make this a wonderful day.'

THE WORK OF CRYSTALS

Archangel Raphael

'This is an auspicious day. For once you are gathered in the presence of the most holy. You must know that there is a special energy that surrounds you and protects you and that raises your vibrations. So whatever you do ask for it as if it was being given to you, not immediately of course, but it will come in increments and you will be different after these sessions. This is a very holy chapel and you did remark upon it when you entered, Mary. It is time now that we are still and listen to what our hearts are asking of us.

I will put you at ease in telling you that my name is Raphael and I came to you yesterday, yes, it was yesterday. You were driving to the airport were you not and I believe you were very much lost in the story that I was unravelling for a young man who is more than worthy and has been left in the shadows long enough and thanks to your gift, you brought him out and I was able to talk to him and tell him who he is. More of that work we will be doing. Now there is no reason in saying: "But couldn't it be faster: we have the facility, we're waiting for the guests?", and I will say to you it would endanger the work of the crystals if you were to bring too many people onto this island at random. The crystal is already trying to deal with the energy of the workmen who are not as aligned as you are and have no idea that this is a special place. We want to make it obvious to those who will come in a year and a half's time that this is a special place and it is sacred and they must come with a proper alignment. If they do not have it, and you will know it just from their names and the vibration of the names, you are not to allow them to come here even to deliver packages, for we have carefully screened those who are here and those who are meant to stay will stay and those who are not able to sustain the extraordinary energy that is coming in will feel very uncomfortable because all of you are learning to grow with it and your systems are being aligned to what it is that is about to happen here because this will be the place of miracles, something that nobody has expected will happen. It will have to do with the spaceships.

We do not want to put you in danger so we are not allowing this to happen too soon but the spaceships will be visible here first of all. The other places are not politically ready and would cause great suspicion to arise around you and you would be treated as outcasts. I do believe you have had enough of those problems and do not want to have to start over with new centres and new energy forms. We will do everything to protect you and the crystal, for we could not carry on the work that we do without the energy from that crystal, without your alignment and knowing that you have signed up for the task that we have given you.

You are working with us at night – each one of you – and working not just as a traditional or humdrum type of job; your job is becoming very fascinating to you and that may be a topic for another session. I could deal with that in more depth but, at present, I think we would like to just make you all aware of what's going on in and around the island and how you are feeling about it for I do want to hear from you.

You may ask your questions but, as you do, I want to know how you are feeling in your emotional bodies: are you feeling comfortable; are you feeling challenged by something that may be difficult; is there any help that you need personally? Too often people have an opportunity to reach deeply into their souls and to ask about questions that could regard their evolution and yet they hesitate saying: "This is not the moment and goodness knows I will take time away from someone else.

113

Three of you, actually two of you, interest me very much and I would like to hear from you. How do you feel in your emotions?" The very fact that you will be dealing in emotional centres, crystals that you have brought into each one of these centres are aligned to the emotions and, as you are clear with your emotions, your feelings, anxiety, fear, anguish, anything that might come up – it needs to be dealt with before others come in. They will walk in and instantly know there is a difference in the energy and they will look to you as carriers of that energy, so different individuals will reflect a different aspect to them and will awaken another chakra. Mary, for example, is to deal with her throat chakra, the one that gives her the most amount of trouble.

So, all of you have your purpose and some of you have not even begun to scratch the surface. We are here today to ask and to enquire as to what you would be comfortable with and how best you would like to start. I know you have a question somewhere about yourself so would you like to ask it please?'

'What could you suggest to open me to my spiritual past; what would be a course of practice, a course of action?'

'Excellent and I apologise; I have not introduced myself, I believe. I am Raphael. I come to you from a very high dimension and I do not usually interact with humans for I have not found them as compliant or obedient or as interesting as you are and that is why I have chosen to give up my anonymity. I am not related to Archangel Raphael. So that there may be no confusion, you may just refer to me as Raphael. Now, as for your request, I take this very seriously and I wish you would do so, as well. If you do not do your daily exercises I would not be offended, but if you would tend to skip these exercises I would say then you do not want to proceed on your path. It is the easiest of the exercises that could be done simply by sitting and breathing and Mary will teach you how to do it and do it with you for she did it for a number of months, in fact we could say over a year, every day, and that has brought her great comfort, an easy ability to align her chakras.

It is your chakras, my dear, that are out of balance and Mary is not allowed to do healings until the month of November, but come November, she will work on you gladly and, perhaps, your friend might want to practice his skills in working and aligning your chakras and he might be amazed and you might want to know that there are interesting things that are happening. So, as you do the breathing exercises, try to find a comfortable position, if possible, when you come home from work for this would relax you very pleasantly. It would not distract you hopefully from your daily tasks and if you do not find the time when you come home then perhaps when you wake up in the middle of the night. Many people find that a good time; they often get up and go to the bathroom and come back and they are half awake but enough so that this would become a synchronised effort.

Once you start the programme, then it would be very easy. It does replace meditation in a sense that you are doing a more profound, active meditation – it is not a passive one – and, as you visualise breathing in light through the centre of your heart, bring in that light, see it as a beacon of light much as something that would come from a lighthouse and, as it penetrates into you, let it work and bring that soothing energy and let it enlarge the heart qualities and all that you would like to project, for know, my dear, that as you set your intent, it is that powerful. You may realise it but without an intent, a definite defined and well thought over intent, you will tend to wobble in your focus and as you are so gifted, you may be drawn into one path and someone calls you, it's an emergency, we need you and you drop everything to help others. This will keep you aligned to your purpose in bringing in your spirituality and if you do nothing more and forget all about Spirit the rest of the day, it won't matter, but we can say now two to three months of doing this on a daily basis will align you to the point where you will be ready to channel and you shall be a channel my dear, and if you think you are helping people now, you will help them far more profoundly in that other space.

115

Now it is a question of doing and you are taking your computer and readying it and doing something with facts or figures or you are writing out notices. Whatever you are doing involves doing – this will involve being and at this point in time there is nothing more important than dealing with beingness and the art of being, being comfortable, being in the awareness of who you are, being your majestic and glorious self and you will not have to tell people who you are; you will stand in their presence and they will say: "I know you; I have known you before as an angel and, yea, even as an archangel". You are that powerful and many have perhaps told you other compliments but this is the truth.'

'Thank you. Is there any message for us today, in particular a special message?'

'Yes, I do thank you for that for you know that we are looking after you constantly; you know that you are presently here in this chapel awaiting to align yourselves to us. I can say since the last time that Mary was here, there has been a significant change. She was a bit disappointed upon arriving because the energy was not quite what she had expected as it was before. Now, mind you, that is not a bad thing. It does not mean that we have gone into hiding nor have we captured all the energy and said you may not have it back – it is simply occupied elsewhere and as you do know, you were evolving from a third dimensional space into a fifth dimensional space.

Well, if you can figure that the crystal has done what it can do on this level, certainly it is not ready to deal with the drug problem on the islands. It has a higher purpose: it is working on the plan. If you can imagine an architect's drawing in blue upon a white paper, it is only written as a skein on the tapestry of time, but it is there as a plan and that crystal is activating points in that plan; it is very busy dealing with the fifth dimension as it will be in this area when you will come back from your abode out on another planet. It means that this is a spiritual centre for Planet Earth and that is why we are

116

stressing the point that only those spiritually evolved souls may be allowed on this space. It is more than sacred and I cannot stress that loudly enough. That is why you have positioned your earth-keeper in a place where there is not only a vortex here but there is one out there in the bay that is protecting it and looking after another one in this bay and how is it, coincidence of coincidences, you are in the middle? Well, my dear friends, we checked you out, we looked into you with great introspection, discovering who your longings were aligned to and what were the most important things that you could do and what you wanted to do. We found that very profound, spiritual base for all of you. So, we knew that it was a place that would be protected. An island is not an easy access for most people and if you were interested, you would allow yourselves to know that not everybody is permitted to come here and then the earth-keeper came and that was the end of our research activity. We did activate it above and beyond any of the other crystals; the ones in the Isle are extremely active in another domain.

This crystal is working with all dimensions and it is working with all of your history, the Atlantian era, the era of the Pacific Isle of Lemuria, of all those powerful energies that have ever been known around this area and, as it is breathing those energies – the good ones, the positive ones that were brought in – it is bringing them back and allowing them, as a fruit tree would: you nourish the roots, you get the food into the base of the tree and you allow it to grow up into the sap and, as a result, you are feeding the branches at the top. Now, all of you will come back, perhaps, if you so choose to and find this place magnificent. Well, what you will see will be the top of the tree. You will not know about the nourishment that was given to the roots nor what kind of vitamins or minerals went up that trunk into the sap of the tree, but we know and we understand that it had to start at the basis of the very root of the energy that has been exploited in this area, and so much has been done: much you know of, much you do not know of and that is what the crystal is occupied with at present. It is not in a negative band of energy as it was. It is as much alive as you

117

are: setting its intent to simply be used to raise those vibrations, to print them onto this plan so that those who come and have the visual ability to see into the threads of time, they will be able to bring that vision to the people who are here and explain to them what it is that has happened and how best they can benefit from that energy.

One might be interested in raising the Atlantian energy; another one might say: "But the spaceships were here therefore I want to tune in to that spaceship energy", another one might say: "But all those energies that were so confused: I would like to know what happened then, and I would like to work with that and sort it out so that it may be remembered as a time of a pivotal energy shift", and that is again another point to tell you that the purpose was preparing this energy, and it did tend to throw compasses off because it was so powerful and it was bringing up old energy which was meeting with the new energy and they did not fit; they coincided and they crashed. None of these souls were forgotten. On the contrary, they have been evolving very rapidly since then. They are working with you and around you and know what your purpose is so that you might see them appear in the water. You might look into the water one day and see a face and as that face comes close, you might want to tune into it and ask it if it is coming to support you, to be helpful, beneficial. If you do get an affirmative answer then you would like to hear from that soul, I am sure. These are, perhaps, threads that you were not that interested in. I could not help myself for it is also something we do with love and passion and we enjoy sharing our knowledge with you. Is there another question you have?'

'Thank you, Raphael. How can my friend go forward with his healing ability and should he be working on that right now?'

'Indeed, it is very important that you work on it; it is the next step and it is allowing you to physically be present in the energy of people. You have aligned yourselves so that you may bring in Spirit magnificently. Now we are asking you to

118

align yourselves in such a way so that you bring in Spirit to work with these subtle bodies of the patients who come to you. Now you may not know of your specialities, what you do best or what it is that you would need to do on each individual, but your energy has grown so pure that merely walking into the energetic field of a patient is enough to bring in a Guide or two, but perhaps you would learn an invocation from Mary. It would be best that you not just walk in to someone's energy field, and do it innocently, for fear that there might be an interruption of that energy and an astral band might have picked up on it. We do say you are protected but we would like to know that you go through the precautions of asking for that protection and that you bring in whatever Guide you would like to come work on this person and that you will introduce your energy gently into their body; look to the spot that you are attracted to, they might complain of a stomach ache but your energy system will say that it is not the stomach that is bothering them, it is a backache and you will try to gently put your hand under that backache where you feel that point and the other hand on top and you will enjoy this. It might be a knee ache in which case it might be the knee so, if you could ask your Guide to channel quietly to you as you are healing, they will explain to you if you are on the right place or if there is another spot to move to. You are beginning your career and you have the benefit of not having lost time in learning assorted methods in different schools and if you are properly prepared, you could not harm anyone as long as you have aligned yourself with your invocation and your intent. So, Mary would be happy to help you out. Is there another question?'

'How can Mary go forward with her healing abilities?'

'Well, it's at a standstill at this point and it is not meant to be worked on. I know she is very concerned about a relative who is, alas, fading because of lack of nourishment more than anything else and if she would cease the chemotherapy, she could perhaps begin to re-establish herself and at least get

119

grounded if she desires to live. Then she would have the capabilities of doing so but by going on with this chemotherapy she is detaching, her soul is detaching, from this Earth plain and there is no other choice for she has assimilated Earth with pain and with not being able to accomplish what she wishes, which is most sad and frustrating. If you all could praise the Lord and ask for a miracle, that it would allow her to stay alive at least until November when Mary will be allowed to go back and work on her, then that would perhaps be fulfilled. So, after this session, if you could quietly sit and close your eyes and pray – whatever way you desire and whatever way you wish – we could bring in that energy and try to visualise her relative. Please explain what she looks like and you could work on her energetically here, sending her the love and the courage to live for another few months then, as we say, "Thy will be done", and the Holy Father will intercede. Was there a question about the earth-keeper?'

'How is the earth-keeper doing? Please explain and is there anything that we can do?'

'Yes, there is a part of what you can do to encourage this crystal and I am glad you asked it. At this point, it is still involved with working on those other dimensions, but it might be time to bring it back to concentrate on you and, in order to do so, I think a bath would be very helpful and after the bath and it has been cleansed and purified, then you may go up and assist it. It would be nice if each of you would hold the crystal on one side and bring in as much love as you can and surround it with love; bring the light out; imagine it exploding in a light force which is healing and beneficial and allowing it to adjust to the softest of energies. It would be a rest period for the crystal, as well, and it has been working very hard. So, if you would choose to do that – perhaps Monday when you are all back together again – that would be very nice providing you do not have time today, whatever is your plan, otherwise I have nothing more for you and I thank you for allowing me to come and be in your midst and to glory in your presence.'

120

'Thank you.'

'So we shall be back again whenever the time is appropriate.'

DISCERNMENT CONCERNING ALIEN SHIPS

Kuthumi

'It's so wonderful to have this place actually working. I thank you, dear Mary, for having such wonderful people over here and thanks for calling out for me.'

'It's such a pleasure to have you, Kuthumi, and to know that you could give them such loving information and support and aligning them with their purpose. Thank you very much. My friend and I wanted to know what happened last night to both of us. Could you explain it?'

'Yes, dear one. It's so wise of you to know and to see what's going on and to actually realise you didn't belong in that enemy spaceship and I thank you for being so prompt and alert to your self conscience that you didn't let them work on you. That was very wise of you, dear Mary. What they were trying to do was to plant a seed in you so wherever you went, they could keep track of you at all times – even when you were on our ship. So, dear one, I thank you and all our commanders are cheering you that you actually got out of there without any serious damage.'

'It looked so familiar Kuthumi.'

'They're good at faking things, dear one, and they tried

122

many, many years ago to catch one of us and they actually got a brain transplanted into one of theirs and they stole some of our technology and knowledge, learning what we do work with and what we don't, but they can never fulfil the love that you always feel in a bright ship that works with our Holy Ones and you will know that when you get in there as you very wisely did. Yes, well done, dear Mary.'

'I asked them for the name of the commander or the ship and I didn't know either so if they had answered me I would probably have been more puzzled.'

'Well, there was a reason why they asked you and you did not give it to them and that's because they don't know how to communicate like we do through our Higher Self.'

'Thank you. Is there a danger tonight? Is it wise for my friend and myself to go out tonight?'

'No. I would not suggest to either one of you to go out tonight. Just practice your meditation or even just a prayer before you go to sleep and just ask the Holy Father to guide you and protect you at all times saying that you are one of his children and he will make sure that you will be all right in your sleeping stage.'

'Thank you. Is there anything special that my friend needs to know about what happened to him last night?'

'Yes. They, too, were trying to take him away. On his journey, as he was planning to go through, he came to the conclusion that it's uplifting. As they saw him progressing, they tried to hold him down – they don't like to see the Star Seeds shining up above, it's almost like attacking them. Yes, they came very close to him but, wisely again, he did use his self conscience to come back and it was a frightening moment, yes indeed, but well done, dear one, and keep your good work up. At all times, when you see them coming to you, just put your hands

123

up and ask for the Holy Father – that you didn't do – but very wisely you did manage to push them away. Like I asked you to do before, with one hand up, and with the other one just push him away as far as you can and they will vanish for life and then bring that wonderful holy light in that we asked you to do. So, all the time, when you feel that fear, put up your guard.'

'Thank you. My friend said that this afternoon he saw what looked light a shadow in the great hall. Is there any danger going on within the house?'

'There is no danger at all but you can see how busy they are trying to get to that wonderful light you carry. They just came through, they could not stop; they cannot stay in that wonderful place that you call home. Not to worry, they will go through but they cannot stay long.'

'And they cannot reach me in my sleep, for example?'

'No, as long as you have with you your Higher Self they cannot do anything to you.'

'Wonderful. We were just going to ask if there is any negative energy coming towards us or coming in that we would have to be prepared for aside from what you have just told us or is that enough?'

'That will do actually and it's not your fault, don't blame yourself for one minute. As you are beaming up the wonderful light that is coming through you, they can see you clearly and they try to bring you back down or then capture you for their side. By all means never give up. Always ask for the Holy Father to guide you and only you. Through your heart you will know – as you did very wisely – and you will just be protected by Him. If you find it is necessary before you go to bed at night, with a little bit of holy water just make a little cross on your forehead and all the time that that cross is there you will sleep at ease.'

'Well I think you have answered all of our questions. We have no others, except, Kuthumi, is there anything else we need to know for this weekend or in preparation for anything?'

'What I ask of both of you – if you have the time, and you will enjoy this very much – is to just go by the crystal again and thank it for its support and say: "Dear one, please protect us at all times and let your wonderful light shine on us brighter and brighter; even if we are falling down, let your wonderful light shine and pick us back up because we together will become united".'

'Last night I went out and I brought the light in and I magnified it and I had such a good time but I'm afraid I just signalled our presence to the negative ones and that was not wise.'

'Not to worry. As I've said before, as your beams are lighting up brighter and brighter, it becomes easier for them to find you. So, as you become brighter, it's wise to be in line with your right Guide at all times and just have faith that God is there to protect you and He will be.'

'Good. Kuthumi, may we check in again tomorrow to find out what we are to do over the weekend?'

'By all means.'

'Thank you.'

'I may leave you all in peace and, dear one, I congratulate you and, please, dear Mary, keep up your wonderful work and energy that you are using with such wonderful beings. I thank you and now I go.'

* * *

'Good morning. It is Kuthumi?'

'Yes, indeed.'

'May I just say to you that what I am feeling now is that we are becoming more and more like little children. We look forward to each moment we can spend with you and we rejoice when we can come and the hours seem to drag when we are away from you. Is this normal?'

'Children, you will be, dear ones, as you are the children of the Holy Father. I beg you to carry on with your duties as you have been doing so wisely and so carefully. Dear Mary, how can I lift up your heart in the same way you have been doing for others? I was told to give you this message this morning: you are being blessed by our Holy One and, by all means, carry on your wonderful work that you are doing. I beg you, at all times, to be connected to your Higher Self and always make those wonderful decisions as you have been doing so wisely by checking in to your Higher Self. I thank you.
Dear Mary, in the same way you love all those wonderful children around you and become that wonderful child that we all see in you then that Light Being will grow brighter and brighter as you always have been. Yes, dear one, by all means, every time you feel down just call on us and, for example, just put both hands out and hold that energy around your heart and feel love and, with your third eye, concentrate on the Holy Father to bring that love to you. You belong to him and he will guide you that way.'

'Thank you Kuthumi. Why do neither Mary nor her friend remember anything from last night? Is there something that we need to know?'

'No, dear one. It was time for your bodies to be at peace. If you could see how much you have been going through, it is like a roller coaster, if you like to call it that way; you've been going and coming so frequently that you did need a rest and we gave that to you but promise you will be very busy in the next few days. It was very wise of you to get an early sleep.'

'We appreciate that, Kuthumi. I also noticed when my friend came in this morning that he looked different: there was an aura about him, he was seeming to be taller, stronger, handsome. I didn't know if something had gone on last night or has it just been an accumulation of his work that is shining through?'

'It is very wise you see that because you are actually seeing what you are becoming; likewise, dear one. So, it is all the wonderful work that you have created and, as he has been doing, always stay in line. It's so important and you can see what is beginning to happen to both of you. The more you do for the Holy Father, the better you feel about yourself and the better others will see that, but only the wise ones like you can see that in the wonderful change that has occurred, and it will carry on. So it is very wise of you to see that dear one, but please, by all means, carry on with your wonderful work in line at all times.'

'My friend also has some pain in his back that seems to be the result of having caught a cold. Is there anything special he could do over the weekend to remove the pain?'

'The ideal thing would be a steam bath but it could be dangerous if he does take the steam bath and catch cold or a draught: it will create more problems, but if he can have a very hot bath and be rubbed with some lotion – just one that removes cold from the back – then right after that have a quick cold shower. That will release that cold energy out of his back and then, by all means, not to go in a draught for at least eight hours and he will be all right.'

'Beautiful, thank you ... Doctor Kuthumi! Do we have any

127

assignments for the weekend? I know I felt this morning I had an assignment.'

'And you're on your way, dear, actually. There was this wonderful being that actually forgot the wonderful words that you have created with him. Please, by all means, just remind him how much light he still has and it is up to him to follow through – don't force anything on him, just remind him.'

'Wonderful, thank you. I think we have no other questions. Yes, there is something else? Do you want us to be out at the crystal today or do you want us to meet again tonight at 9.00 or Sunday night? What is best?'

'If possible today – whatever time is convenient to both of you – to go there by the crystal and just make it feel part of you and you will notice the energy completely change. So please, by all means, go there and, if you like to call it that, "charge yourselves", charge those wonderful Light Beings that you both are and wherever you walk, make it walk with you; let that Light Being be your sight and your Guide. This is your source and it will be your wisdom. Go forward with it at all times, and other people will see that wonderful energy that is coming from you. It is not yours to give and it is not for them to receive it from you, it is for them to ask for the Holy Father or, likewise, do the wonderful work that you are both doing and they, too, will carry that remarkable energy and spread it.'

'That's beautiful and tonight: do we go out to the ship again?'

'Tomorrow night, dear one.'

'Is the negativity being released?'

'Yes.'

'Thank you. I felt it was calmer last night and I can meditate again.'

'By all means. Thank you for making this wonderful effort to come here to visit with me and around here. As you probably noticed, there are more than one here this morning, that's why the energy feels so great for all of you. I beg you to take this energy and share it, walk with it and all times, feel it in your heart. If you ever feel down or lonely, just call upon us and say: "Dear Father, can I have that wonderful energy that I received at the chapel?". Please do this by all means, and ask only that those who serve may come with me. I beg you to go in peace and have a wonderful journey. Amen.'

'Amen.'

'Along with Kuthumi I bless you and tell you my name is Skakus. I have come this morning because I see that there is another piece that is needing to be given to you. I feel you are working more than we had ever expected of any of our devotees. We call you devotees and not disciples for your devotion to Spirit has been exemplary. Many disciples are doing the work and doing it because they are feeling good about their work and about the connection to the Holy Father and, yet, there is pride in their work and their accomplishments. We have seen none of that in either of you and that is why we wish to come to call you devotees and, of course, if you are a devotee, you are a devotee of the Holy Father and none other and your allegiance has been pure, has been wondrous and there is nothing – not a stone nor a pebble – left unturned where we have asked you to do something and you have not done it. It has been as perfect as humans can be and we do not wish you to leave this chapel this morning dispirited, discouraged or feeling that perhaps you have not done enough or perhaps there was something that you missed that you could have done better. Let me tell you this morning, there is nothing you could have done better than you have done. You have been prudent when it was required; you have been courageous when we asked you to be and you have been daring, daring to get into a ship, daring to leave your bodies, daring to be present when the Almighty Father has called you. I am not saying because I am Skakus that I am ordering you to come. If I ask you it is because the Holy Father has asked me to ask you and it does not mean that he cannot give you the message directly, of course he can, but we are part of a family and as the essence of the family needs to grow in interacting with one another. Imagine yourselves on a soccer field or playing a game, you need to know who will pass you the ball when you need it most because you are well positioned in front of the goal. It is not letting them take it and rushing to the goal and being tackled and knocked down and you lose your opportunity. I am saying that now you are realising when it is time for you to take action and being bold and when it is time for you to pass the ball so that the other team-mate can do it. Do you see, it is very intricate; we are part of a team and this team is extremely important. We have direct access to the Holy Father and you may not have known it but one day you were channelling the Holy Father and we did not tell you at the moment though Mary tried to because you would have faltered and fallen apart, but it is possible. Your connection has grown so pure and so beautiful and the light around you is sparkling on our level at a ratio and a frequency that we have rarely seen amongst humans.

Priests often become discouraged and earth-bound; they forget that their place is there on the other side and if they disconnect too much, they cannot carry out their functions and it becomes a timepiece; put the incense out at the proper time, ring the bells, pour the wine, do this, do that. Do you see, their functions hold them down and it does not allow these Light Bodies of spiritual energy to flow. You do have your times when you and Mary can sit and be with us and can energise that battery that is there inside your heart, that is waiting to be fed and to be nourished and, perhaps, put in the right mixture of oil and gasoline so that it will not put her out – excuse the expression – I am not adapted to the present day vocabulary.

I wish to give Mary a message. The work we are doing

130

together is not meant to discourage her though I am seeing more and more as we are growing to be a team that it is difficult for her to wake up in the morning with great energy and excitement. That inner glow that she was carrying she has left it with me and this is not what the Holy Father wants of us. So, more and more we will have to align our energies so that I am present with her at times and will be working with her and through her when she is with groups, so, in that way, she does not feel that I have come and abandoned her again. This is again an abandonment issue though it had its reason for her and for me and that this time I am being asked by the Holy Father to nourish that part of her soul that is feeling it is shifting to be another case of abandonment. She has lived through that in many lifetimes. This is not something that could be healed by going to one or two of a therapist's classes – it is something that has been happening to her regularly as part of her learning process. She needed to draw upon her spirituality herself and not lean upon others but this time, in her plan and in her purpose, it is so critical that if I was to come and go as I have been doing, I would abandon her again and the disappointment would be too much for her heart to carry right now.

So, she is asking to be removed and to be taken to a space where she and I can interact regularly, and the Holy Father is saying no not yet. We need her energy upon this planet and, especially, a female energy which is soft and welcoming and mother-like because without that, then it becomes again strict and condemning, and that is what the church has represented for many: putting people down, blaming, crying out sin, unfaithfulness and people are trying to comply. We are asking of you to merely give the heart up to the Holy Father and let that heart be blessed and become a shining, radiant point of light within each being. The ones who will start this message will be the Star Seeds, much as the ones who came yesterday and when they understand that their heart is like a lightbulb they may turn it on and let the heat and the light and the frequency beam forth from it; they will find many lights coming on and they will be attracting many, many souls, but

131

that will happen – I do not wish to say gradually because nothing is happening to you gradually – but you are moving into a capacity where you are becoming more important – not just to your fellow beings – but to us; critical as pivotal parts of a machine whereby if that machine does not turn properly and move in its orbit, the other pieces will be affected and it will jam at some point.

So, I do not want to see you discouraged; this has been the purpose of my coming and I have not intended to. Kuthumi and I agreed that he would carry the message and when I saw Mary's heart breaking, I had to come and I thank you for being here for there is a part of me that is saddened, as well, and it is something we have shared in many lifetimes away from this planet, away from this part of the universe – in fact, in other universes. So there is much for us to connect with and to form a bonding that needs to take place. The Holy Father is aware of it and it will happen within the next three months but, in the meantime, I ask you to carry on. I see sadness in your heart, as well. Is there something I can do to help?'

'Thank you for being here with us and for sharing that wonderful advice for Mary.'

'And you shall never be left alone my dear. It is not saying to you that your partner, here on this bench, will leave. She will not leave. You two will be taken together. You have made a pact and a bond between each other and that is why your progress has been so grand because you have worked with each other and offered each other the energy you needed and you two shall grow. I know you have been promised much and often when the time came there was another disappointment. If I may put it this way, it was the Holy Father's way of testing you, but tests are not what we are looking at right now. You do not need them any longer, but we do need you to stay here and keep your energy here until you can see some of these Bright Lights able to carry on by themselves.

So, as much as I can ask you to, when you see someone

bright, ask your Guides: "Is this a Star Seed? Is this an angel? Is this a Light Being?", and as you get the answers – especially, for the Star Seeds – try to make an appointment for them to come to the island under any pretext and stop them off just to visit the chapel and awaken their curiosity, so that as they see it and they feel the energy, many angels will be around and around them, so you will not have to always say: "You need to be here tomorrow". It will happen; they will be drawn to it. Others will, unfortunately, choose not to come, but there are enough Star Seeds that are sleeping here that you will have a nice following within three months. So take heart. Are you feeling better?'

'Yes, thank you.'

'We will always be looking after both of you and as we reach out and the Holy Father comes through us to shine his light upon you and to say to you: "You are blessed amongst souls upon the Earth. Take heart, my dear ones, you are not the lost sheep. You are shepherds and we love you". With this blessing I leave you and ask you to go amongst your tasks and your people light hearted and knowing that you carry this beauty, this light, this wondrous love of the Holy Father. I leave you and bless you. Goodbye, my dears.'

* * *

'I am St George and I greet you, my friends. It has been some time since I have come to this chapel. It is a welcome reminder of your beauty and your wonderful energy.'

'Thank you St George. We haven't heard from you for some time. Are you well?'

'Yes, thank you.'

'St George, we come this morning – not confused – but wanting to hear from you and from our Holy Father, what are

133

we to do to organise ourselves. When I got up this morning I saw this beautiful moon setting over the horizon and I heard Skakus saying: "Bring in the Light Beings and the Star Seeds, as many as you can and in three months' time you will have a considerable following". Could you tell me somehow how we are to do this: as a group or do we bring them in individually or do we tell them to come and meet my friends? How would you suggest we do it?'

'Dear one, if you bring them all together it will be very uncomfortable for you and for others. So, by all means, do bring them in as you feel fit and it doesn't have to be all at once. Yes, by bringing them in and just taking them to that wonderful vortex of yours and saying: "This is what we have to offer you; feel the light, dear one, and now it's just like this little star that you see above you", and they'll probably look up and still won't see it and then say to them: "Just imagine now that that wonderful star is shining upon you and you are going to plant that one here, on this vortex, and watch it grow". By doing that with their love and their wonderful energy, they will start to grow and open up. So yes, by all means dear one, do it as is appropriate for you.'

'Thank you St George. I'm not quite clear as to how they bring that? Are they to visualise the star coming down into the crystal?'

'No, they will see it above them first and all of them have that inner sight, as all Star Seeds do, and, as they visualise and get the feeling of that star above them, with their own energy, they will bring it and plant it on the vortex. Let them do it – each individual – or even six or seven could do it, but let them all do their own and you might be there to guide them and tell them exactly what has happened to them.'

'So it would be better as a group and not as individuals?'

'Right.'

'Thank you. I could even do that with a group of the teachers who are coming in.'

'That would be very wise of you to do that.'

'Thank you St George. I believe that I understood on Sunday when I spoke to Skakus that in two weeks' time we are going to have a considerable onslaught of negative energy and that perhaps my understanding was wrong but I heard that my friend and I didn't need to go through it. What I am concerned about is that my friends are coming on the 27th which would be precisely at the same time. Is it better that I tell them not to come or to come at a later date or do we change our plans in any way? What do we do?'

'No, dear one. Carry on with the way your plans are and do whatever you have to do in that matter and perhaps what I would like to see both of you doing, seeing as you are on almost a different level at this moment, is to share your energy with them but, before you do that, dear one, make sure that what you are sharing is not for them to keep or hold on to. Your energy surrounded by the energy here will work clockwise and visualise a tornado, if you like, and see it just going up further and further away. Now, as that light goes up don't give it away to just anyone, but see if you can reach the Higher Self, and just concentrate and pray at the same time you do this. This light is for the Holy Father only and when it reaches that wonderful energy it should come like a cloud of little bright lights, just shining right through this wonderful energy and surround you and your friends. All of you will be doing this wonderful work and you will feel so light, so happy that you will carry it with you wherever you go.'

'Is this a form of protection?'

'Yes but the protection is the one that you actually created and it was blessed by the Holy Father and sent back to you.'

'And do we do this once a day?'

'Just once will be great; you don't have to do it any more than that. You just have to do it once wherever it is appropriate for you.'

'And would it be better to do it out around the crystal or here in the chapel?'

'You can start it here in the chapel by just meditating for fifteen to twenty minutes and then go to the crystal. That way your conscience is actually clear. Go to the crystal and do this wonderful work.'

'Thank you St George. So the date will be given to us when we are to do that?'

'Yes.'

'So do I tell my friends about this negative energy or is it preferable not to?'

'Wait until they come here and then talk to them.'

'Thank you very much St George. Have you a message for my friend?'

'It is for him to do all over again what he did on Saturday and then he will be back on his feet full of light and energy. Thank you, dear Mary, and may you both go and have a wonderful day and I just beg you all to be Light Spirits just like our Holy Father always tells us to be even if we forget it sometimes. Go in peace. Amen.'

BEING STRONG AND ENERGISING YOUR BODY

St George

'I am St George. It's wonderful to be here and it's such a beautiful day. It has been a long time and again, I thank you. Yes dear one?'

'Have you anything in particular to say to us; what our evolution is and is there something we need to do?'

'Be strong; energise your bodies to a certain extent that no harm will come in to you by doing this work dear one. If you can get your chakras to work on a regular basis in the morning or evening – whichever is good for you – charge them up and with this wonderful charge that you are bringing in: surround yourself by it, fill yourself with it, and you will be walking on air with the wonderful energy that you feel. It's the one that is coming from you and, as you walk by negative energy, yours will be so powerful that nothing can outshine it.

You will be like a mirror and any of that energy that comes in contact with it will automatically reflect back the way it came from and you will walk a lot lighter, a lot healthier, but do it yourself, fill yourself first. As I say, whenever it is convenient for you. I would suggest in the morning before you make that first step, when you make your first appointment to meet anyone that you are going to meet – fulfil yourself. It's

137

like having breakfast and you shall see the difference, you will be lighter and healthier. Thank you for listening.'

'Thank you. Could you tell us, or could you tell me please, is the pain that I am going through all part of my transition and is it something I need to surrender to?'

'It is a transition you are going through, surrendering; it's okay but if you do surrender, please surrender pain not your loving energy. What I would like to see you do is discharge whatever the pain is that you feel in any part of your body. Take that negative energy out – you can do it or you can ask your friend to do it – and fill with positive, good energy along with the bright light. Ask to be purified and by being purified, any changes that occur in your body will not feel like pain. Give yourself up only to the Holy One, not to negative energy. If you give yourself to the negative energy, then more negative energy will come into you.'

'Well, the other day I felt my knee go out. It's gone out several times and now my hip has gone out of place. Is that negative energy?'

'You have been walking on some of that negative energy and automatically you have been trying to stop it – not knowingly – but your spiritual mind is trying to stop it and only by doing that, i.e. stepping on the negative energy, you collapse onto that vibrational frequency. Your defences are down and the negative energy comes in and takes over. But know that you can walk free anywhere you like without picking up any of that negative energy. Fill yourself with Light and Love and nothing can touch you. It's very important for humans to recognise how easily we forget how singular we are and as we walk not thinking we are on some level allowing that negative energy to take over. When the pain comes then that's the time we start to pray and ask for miracles; that you could have done before it happened. Protect yourself first, light up, and fill yourself with the wonderful gift that our Holy

Father gave to us when we were little. Purified, it almost cleans your body and fills you with that incredible light and love that God has given to all mankind.'

'Beautiful, thank you. We wanted to ask this afternoon if we are to use hypnosis as therapy. Is that something you could recommend to us?'

'It's fine to work with hypnotism but I would not suggest that you mix it up with spiritual healing for otherwise they will think spiritual healing is putting someone into a hypnotic trance. If you have been under hypnosis you don't remember what transpired. They will think it is nonsense, it's like an electrician substituting for a magician. Please do not mix them up whatever you do.'

'Not even to use it to help people overcome bad smoking habits?'

'Not to mix with the spiritual work; separately, yes. If you want to have a session, you can work independently on any bad habits whatsoever. Please make a different time and date but not in the same context as you do your spiritual healing. Please, whatever you do, don't mix them both together.'

'So you wouldn't recommend hypnosis then in general?'

'Not to mix it with the spiritual work that you are doing.'

'Thank you; that's deeply appreciated. What is it I can do to help my friend in his healing ability? Is there anything I can do?'

'One good thing will be to show him the parts of the human body; for example, explain how you have them on a skeleton and show him exactly where the parts go so he will be more aware. Even the Guides will tell him exactly what to do. He should know where to go before the Guides move his hands on the body or wherever that problem is. It is always good that he has a clear vision from the standpoint that he knows exactly where to go and he thinks he is going in one direction because he knows that's where the problem should be. Yet the Guide may move his hands in a different direction and to him that will be a lesson that he is not doing the work; it is the Spirit that he asks, the healer, that is doing the work for him, and by doing this sort of exercise he will be a great healer.'

'Will he need, St George, to develop his third eye so he can see blockages?'

'He can already see, when he does the channelling, and you will be amazed at what he will be able to do in a few weeks' time but, at the moment, you will be able to do this for him and get him to work on anyone: brother, sister, you, anyone and see how he does it. He will be quite surprised and so will those that he will heal. He will be finally climbing the ladder and one day he will be up there with the rest of us, shining with us in harmony.'

'I almost feel he is already there. St George, is it right for me to give him the invocation I use to start the healing?'

'It's a good way of doing it because it prepares your body to receive the healers and the beautiful Spirits that come down to do the healing for you; that's a good way of doing it. The other way is he can do it in channelling but get him to open his eyes. That's one of the most powerful things that he should try to do, to open his eyes while you are doing the channelling and if he can do that he will be able to see right through that person like an x-ray vision because his energy and his love will attract the healing Guides to go there and work with the human's heart that heals almost the entire body.'

'Is it a good way to start helping him by bringing in the channelling, through imagining a golden ball above his head and allowing it to come down that way or does he need to use his present system and just open his eyes once he has received his Guide?'

'Then he is ready to start the healing and just get him to open his eyes, but not to lose the magnet, don't lose the love that he is sharing when he has the Guides in. Always keep contact and well grounded and he will feel incredible energy and so will whoever the person he is working on. Thank you for being there for him.'

'I am always there for him as I feel he is for me. Thank you St George. I was told I was not to do any healing until the month of November. Is that correct?'

'To others maybe not, but to yourself, dear one, I can see now you need to rest. At the same time activate the third eye and please, do work on yourself. You should have your vision a lot sooner than you think by healing yourself and this matter of healing yourself doesn't mean losing your energy, no, put extra energy into you and whatever part of the body that you feel needs it the most but, don't just take that little bit of energy and put it there. Make sure your bodies are completely filled and you will see this energy just glowing whiter and whiter around you. It is almost like you can grab the very thin air but that thin air is so powerful that you can hold it together and you can just put that energy wherever you want it to be. Heal yourself first; it doesn't take that long. After you have healed yourself, you can go out there and heal others but I beg you, take care of yourself first; fill yourself with energy and you will be glowing. Even in the dark we will be able to see you and find you no matter where you are because that energy and the love coming from you is so powerful nothing can touch you and no one can miss you. So please take care of yourself first.'

'If I understand you correctly, am I to bring that energy into my third eye?'

'Not all at once. I would like to see the energy fulfil the body completely and you will feel it expanding and as it does expand, bring it in wherever you want to; just grab it like you grab the air and when you feel the energy between your hands, yes, you can put it on your third eye and you will see right through it and once you open that third eye, bright as it is, dear one, I wish I could be there to see your excitement. Once that is done, nothing can hold you back because you will be able to see the good and the bad automatically because you have the energy and the power to do that but make sure you are filled first before you do any healing on you or anybody else.'

'Dear one, it's nice to have a dear friend around you. They will help you and they will guide you in every way they can but then yet you are yourself. Why have the fear that you need someone to be with you if you know very well you can take care of yourself at all times? If someone has the fear that something is going to happen to them, automatically they will attract the very thing they don't want, but if they open up like that beautiful butterfly and be free as you are free, then make sure you are strong enough that you can fly high enough that, no matter what, nothing can disturb you whereas if you open up very little, you may attract the very thing you don't expect, especially if you are in fear. That fear is not very good because you are not standing on your own two feet and you deserve more than just being there as a pet. You are no pet. You have freedom and your freedom comes from you, your strength and once you have recharged your body, please, dear one, make sure you are protected with your beautiful white light and you will be stronger than ever but you have to do that yourself.'

'That feels very good and right. Thank you.'

'May our Holy Father leave you all in peace and may no one ever harm you in any way. Our Holy Father loves you all and even when I am gone, our Father is always looking on all of His wonderful light stars and bright seeds. Now, go in peace. Amen.'

142

DESCRIBING THE HOLY ISLAND

Sananda

'Good evening. Welcome.'

'Thank you.'

'And congratulations.'

'Thank you once again.'

'It's so nice to be back.'

'We welcome you Jesus: if I may call you Sananda?'

'Yes, by all means.'

'Thank you. We have some questions tonight and wanted, first of all, to thank you for returning the island to us. Is it true that it is the property of the most Holy Fathers?'

'Indeed. Everything that our Father created is holy. This is holy in a closer sense: purposeful. It's like a centre all around you, all the land, it's holy and this particular spot is the centre of the holy ground.'

'Thank you. We want to be sure that we are doing the right

143

thing according to you, the Ascended Masters, to the Holy Father. Is there something, a direction, that we need to take or something special we need to do now?'

'Yes, you are doing the right thing, in particular what you do at night when you go to the space centre. It's good to be connected with those beautiful beings and restore their faith in humans. You, also, come to be with the Ashtar Command and learn from the Space Brothers.'

'Why are we often in pain upon waking up?'

'That pain you are receiving shouldn't be.'

'I thought it was Master Metitron working on me.'

'Even if they work on you, they are so delicate that they should not hurt you and, please, ask for guidance when you go up there to be protected from any pain, that you should not receive any pain while you are doing this type of work.'

'Thank you, thank you. My friend had a question. He wanted to know the purpose of the white light that he sees at night and what can he use it for?'

'That light is powerful if he learns how to use it. He can use it for healing, for energy, to remove pain. That white light is sent by one of his masters, St George, and every time that he sees that white light please do not hold onto it. He will be able to control it by moving from side to side but don't hold onto it, let it be free. By using his conscious mind, he can move it in any direction but don't hold onto it and never keep it inside your body for a very long time – release it. He can use that bright light to help others if they have pain. It's an energy light sent from St George and, one day, he might come to it and use that white light for the help of others.'

'Is it something that he can give to others or, for example, he wanted me to use it but I don't think it's mine, I think it's his?'

'It's not his to give. It belongs to St George.'

'Thank you.'

'St George is welcome to use it for him but he has to release it. It's not a light to hold onto. It doesn't even belong to him, you are just able to use it as a gift, but not to keep.'

'Is there something that my friend and I need to learn right now, something special now that we don't have the worry about the island?'

'Yes, both of you have a lot to learn. Start communicating with your dear friends, your dear ones and start to share the magnificent work that you are doing but only to those that you can trust and those that share the same spiritualism as you do.'

'Good. We don't need to learn anything in particular then?'

'As I say, what you need to learn will come as you meet these people, exchange ideas with one another. The main goal out of this whole thing is to bring everyone you need together as a whole family or a holy family and by getting everyone involved, slowly, but, look at a bunch of fruit in a bowl, if you can get six out of ten or even four out of that fruit to reproduce and go out into the fields, you are doing good because that fruit will go out and reproduce and re-seed itself and you will get good fruit, even though you couldn't get everything in the bowl, at least you managed to save some and this will come with your dear ones and those that you trust and you will bring them all together – it will be like the fruit that you are spreading out into different fields and you shall share the good news with others.'

'Is this something that we ought to do more on the island or just meet people outside the island?'

'Outside, yes, or you can invite them; maybe have a session.'

'Channelling?'

'Yes, but only to those that you have full trust in and by doing that, the channelling you do you will get the message through them what you should be doing with them and with others.'

'Excellent, thank you. I think our last question was to ask if the island was happy?'

'Not just the island is happy but all around it, the water, everything and the energy is so much stronger but, again, don't hold any energy. If you have it, share it, move it around. Energy is supposed to be spread and the more you spread it, the better you feel and better other things will feel: trees, plants, birds, fish – everyone will be happy. If you hold the energy you are being greedy so share it, just go around and spread it and let it float.'

'Thank you, Sananda. I think we have no other questions.'

'Thank you.'

CONNECTING WITH THE VORTEX
AND THE FLOW OF ENERGY

St George

'It's nice to be here. My name is St George. Thank you and welcome.'

'Welcome, welcome St George. What a pleasure to hear from you.'

'Will you carry on with your questions please?'

'Thank you. We would like to know what my associate and I will do when my friends come to visit me. Could you help us with that?'

'It will be nice for the four of you to circle around the vortex and try to connect the vortex with the strongest flow of the energy at the centre of the crystal and hold your hands together; do one session there. You will be told what date and you will surround it with love to strengthen it, the love of the vortex.'

'Is there something we need to repeat: a prayer or whatever we did before?'

'Yes. You can read a copy of the vortex prayer and you can

147

say a prayer. Yes, you can say the prayer of St Francis, that will be very nice.'

'Good. Is there anything else that we need to do together?'

'Yes. You can work. Also find time for playing; do some healing.'

'Could my friend use a healing?'

'Yes he could – both of you.'

'Oh good. Is there any particular subject that we need to work on or a preparation that is required right now?'

'At the moment, by being together, you are uniting yourselves. As you go up to the crystal, it will be like uniting yourselves together, ready for the next vortex.'

'Wonderful. Thank you very much St George. Is there anything more about the period from the 20th March until the 5th April?'

'Just be loved and show it to those who you come in contact with – the love that comes from the heart.'

'I can feel it in me right now.'

'Thank you. If you can make others feel that way it will be a much better place for the universe.'

'Could you perhaps help us to know what kind of work we need to do when we are together with our friends?'

'Healing is number one.'

'Are we all to see my Doctor?'

'Your friend from Europe should see him: she needs to see

him but the rest of you don't. If you work together in this healing session you will feel light, you will feel loved. You have to remember to feel something; you have to give it first and you will automatically get it. If it is love, if it is strength that you are needing, give some of that strength away but do not empty yourselves, your reserves. It is a question of not holding on to or over-protecting a part of yourself that needs to open. Here you can just be yourself and then you shall see great things will happen, not just to you but to all those around you.'

'I can see it as a healer that I would like to give my love and strength to the patient on the table but how would we do it; just interacting with people?'

'That you are not allowed to do. When you do healing, your love must not touch that person for you will become very emotional and it doesn't serve its purpose. When you do healing, use your Guides, give your love to them and let them deal with that. Through them, they will know what can be done to that person.'

'So, I am not to touch my patients?'

'Yes, you can touch them but the love, send it to the masters that are working with you and let them deal with it.'

'Thank you. The last question I have, St George, is what are we to do in the Isle in July together? Do we need to work on the vortex while we are there and what do we do on the vortex?'

'Re-align those vortices, almost identical to what you have done here and those that are like your babies, they need love and they are very lonely right now but as they are growing, you will be very proud to see the wonders, the beautiful work that they are doing thanks to you – particularly you Mary.'

149

'Do we need to bring over meteors for them?'

'Not out there. You are so close to the North Pole, you won't need them out there.'

'Well tell me, St George, my friend has noticed that it is a milder winter here, on the island, this year. Is it possible it's because of the crystal and the vortex?'

'It's all the work that you are doing, opening these vortices and, as you can see, that will begin to happen in the Isle also but it takes between nine months to a year and none of this will come together until you accomplish all the work that you have to do. Once they are all open, it is like a puzzle: all the pieces are put together. Hopefully after this, no one has anything to worry about but to enjoy it and see the beautiful joy of the angels around us.'

'May I clarify something St George? I am confused about sending love to people. I hear you when you say to send the love up to the Masters but, for example, when I am listening to somebody, I concentrate on their throat chakras and I send love from my third eye and my heart chakra: is that wrong?'

'No, that's okay, that's all right. You need to recognise that a healer is like a doctor: if you show any emotion to that person you are working with, you are going to get mixed vibes back from them and that's not very healthy for you or the patient. If you give the love, you become so weak that you are doing good to the patient but you feel so tired and weak that you just want to collapse because your energy is going to the wrong hands whereas, if you give your love to the masters, they only use what they have to and you feel a lot stronger because they know your strength.'

'Beautiful, thank you. Is there anything that we need to prepare for our time in the Isle in the sense of teaching and the classes that will take place?'

'For that, you should be looking already for teachers and, also, see if you can get the right contacts. Who and what are you going to have to teach? Prepare lists, get them all together, unite them all together but don't get their hopes up that you will necessarily use them. Once you have some names, you can tell them exactly when you are planning to have them working for you. In that case they know what to do and how to go about it to bring the right environment, the right people for the school.'

'I was thinking of using my friends who are coming to visit as teachers and, hopefully, I could learn enough to be one as well. Is that appropriate?'

'For you, yes, but before you start anyone teaching, make sure they are qualified in a certain way.'

'How will I know that?'

'Give them a test and if they pass by you, with your approval, then they are good enough to be teaching.'

'Could we run everyone through a test in July when we are together?'

'All those that will be ready, yes please. If not, start them in a nice way; you want qualified people to run the place for you with no regrets or surprises.'

'Thank you.'

'I was kind of hoping that when the teaching time comes, I could do channelling for it: is that appropriate?'

'It will be and you will be very good at it.'

'Thank you. My friend as well?'

'Yes, in different subjects.

151

'I want to thank you for being here.'

'It's been a pleasure. Do we have any more questions?'

'No, we just wish you would come back again.'

'I certainly will. Thank you both.'

MESSAGE 'TO LIGHT UP' AND
ASK FOR GUIDANCE

Kuthumi

'Greetings, dear Kuthumi and welcome.'

'Thank you dear ones and please, by all means, light up. It is easier said than done but please, by all means, light up – even at night if you have to excuse yourself. Just light up that wonderful candle at your bedside and ask for guidance and at that particular hour and moment you will receive a very important message. Yes, dear Mary?'

'What hour? You mean if we're with other guests or with other people that we need to excuse ourselves and go into our rooms?'

'No, dear one. After you finish your duties, by all means, just come into your house or your room and light up that wonderful candle by your bedside. Try to meditate or channel one of your very important messengers and he will come through very clear to you.'

'Is that true for my friend as well?'

'Likewise, yes.'

'I tried last night Kuthumi and it seemed I couldn't get any Guides.'

'You will get it tonight.'

'Oh, thank you. Do you mind if we ask questions?'

'By all means.'

'Thank you. Of course, my friend and I want to know what we are going through. What are these strange feelings we are having during the day and at night? I think you wanted us to ask our Guides did you not?'

'Yes, by all means.'

'Thank you. I wanted to ask if I was doing the wrong thing to cling to Simeon, the angel, but perhaps again I should ask them?'

'No, that they will be glad to answer, dear. You are not doing the wrong thing by snuggling up to him, but don't hold on to him; he is as free as you are and by holding on to something it will eventually hurt you. So, by all means, snuggle up to him; love him the same way you have done but free and maybe you both will get freedom together and I will leave the rest as a mystery.'

'Thank you Kuthumi. Blessings and I think we have no more questions but we pray we may be able to do that which you have asked us to do with God's love and help.'

'I will be out there watching for both of you tonight and let that wonderful beam shine and, I beg you, to go in light and at all times remember who your Holy Father is – never forget who he is or what you are here for. Amen.'

'Thanks. Could you tell us please when some take on two jobs simultaneously? Isn't that exhausting?'

154

'That is correct for if they are torn between one job and the other – they are hurrying up to finish one and perhaps not doing their very best, so they may rush off to the other job and the next morning they are not as keen and anxious for the new day's workload and it is not meant to be heavy – if they could regard their work with pleasure, with satisfaction. We do see changes happening on the island as to energy and who is pulling at it and who is a contributor. You might see dramatic changes happening even before you come back, for your replacements will be very strict and fair but they will be checking on people regularly – that is part of their assignment, and they will let no loose ends go unravelled. You will find a very tight ship when you come back and people will respect you almost to the point of saluting you. As your energy expands, others, such as Star Seeds, light workers of some sort will be the ones who will attract your attention when they comment on your energy field.'

'Thank you. I would like to know exactly what happened to me last night?'

'It's only fair if you will be part of us very shortly, you do need to know. We took you through the manoeuvres and showed you what it is like when you pilot the plane, so to speak, and not to worry that you are just repairing parts and re-planning and re-configuring the ship, you are also a very good and astute pilot. So we wanted you to feel validated that you were not left out in all of this play world; that you come to a new reality and that you are re-awakened to your talents and your abilities. You are very good at taking us through bumpy paths where there are black holes and where there are difficult passages that have been foreseen, for example, boulders going through the sky. You do not want the spaceship to be bombarded with any kind of boulders so you know others will chart the course, but you will feel instinctively which is the best route to take and, as you know, the starships do take some time to go from one point to another because the universe is so vast. During those times when the others are tired and they

155

have need of a rest period, you are called upon to come in and refresh the plan, to refresh the pilots, to take over – not in a cocky way of saying: "I know better, let me have the controls", you come in in a very gentle way. If you could imagine yourself watching *Star Trek*, who you might be; watch Commander Data and you might be very surprised and tune into his functions as he is always on the Commander's deck and he is always looking at the controls and computing things that no one else has any knowledge of. The same goes for you while you are there doing your work, discreetly, one after another will come to you and ask which is more advisable and when all else fails and they are called elsewhere in the ship, then you are left at the commands and they know that the ship is in the best hands possible.'

'Thank you.'

'So do sparkle today and enjoy the fact that you are someone very critical to all of us and important, someone that we treasure and look forward to being with.'

'Thank you; likewise. Is there anything else special for us today?'

'Well, I do know that Mary was concerned, not concerned but surprised, when she approached Quan Yin to see Quan Yin crying and she wondered if those were tears of despair, of disappointment, of separation of some sort, or if she had done something wrong.'

'Very briefly, Quan Yin said these are tears of sadness; sadness because you are going away and for you it is gladness, but Quan Yin felt that she would be undergoing the loss of separation and sadness at not having that daily contact with Mary, although Mary does not remember it always but she is always with Quan Yin when she does her channelling. She is there watching after her and loving her as no one else has done on this Earth plane.

156

I wish to say my gratitude, as well, to Quan Yin for she has replaced me when I have been out on command duty and no one else was allowed to be around, my dear one and there is no sadness in our hearts; it is emotion, it is a transition that we have looked forward to for so long that there are tears because this is something that we – how can you say it – more that someone gives you a gift that you have longed for since you were a little boy and you wanted it so badly then, whether it was a new bicycle, or if you had lived in the north – a pair of ice-skates or a musical instrument that you wanted to play for some time, and you didn't get it as a child. Then suddenly, someone appeared and said: "We know this is childish, but perhaps we thought you might like this," and you see it and you weep because those tears are remembrances of the days when you did want it so badly and now your Holy Father brings you the gift. So, they are tears of gratitude".'

'Thank you. Why is Mary shaking lately?'

'Well, we do recognise that she observes everything going on and there have been dizzy spells that she has contracted at home, and been in bed as a rule when it has happened, but got up again when she was given the clear signal to go out and about her business. So, yesterday she had moments of shaking and moments of being dizzy – not to the point where she had to excuse herself – but she did need to sit down and it is this happening that I have described so, let it not be a torment to either of you; rejoice when it comes; just be comfortable and know that you are in a very private place for at least fifteen minutes. If you need to disconnect the telephone when you are in your office, we would prefer it and that you would be in a space where the answering machine would not click on or frighten you. If you are in transit and those sounds come to call you back into your body. What will happen is you will evacuate your body – we will take you up in to the starship and there will be a replacement there ready to take on your body, so nothing will transpire that could harm it, and that negative energy will not be allowed to surround either one of you during that period – we have seen to that.

You will have a multitude of what you would refer to as extraterrestrials around you guarding every porthole that could possibly be exposed. You might, perhaps, feel their presence before it happens, but it will not come at a time when you are driving your automobile or your motorcycle or in transit between two spots whereby you cannot sit down and rest. We will be attentive as to the timing for both of you.'

'Thank you for coming in this morning and answering all these questions for us.'

'Are there other concerns you might have as to how your replacement will know what to do?'

'For that I have trust in you, thank you.'

'That is beautiful and we honour you for that . . . Commander Data!'

'Thank you.'

'And I think you are looking forward to some sort of levity and laughing again and being as the little children that you do know how to be so beautifully. We are pleased and delighted that the Holy Father has given us the permission for we have begged on your behalf that you go at the same time. It was not in the original plan, but the Holy Father did look down upon you and came through you to channel and found that everything we had said was not just true, but was even more beautiful than we had described. So the Holy Father has given his blessing to this and, if you could imagine the four million people in the Philippines saying High Mass to the Pope and with the Pope. Imagine that we are gathered on our spaceships. No for there is not just one spaceship involved with your transition, but many and we are more than four million here to applaud you both and to welcome you. There will be many tears so do not hesitate to let your emotions become apparent to all of us as we applaud you and we rejoice.'

'Thank you. I know we are both looking forward to being there with you.'

'And this time I do not say "Adonai", I say until we meet again and it will be very shortly. So take heart, take courage, go about your job in the most cheerful way you can – not overdoing it of course – but in your usual jolly, pleasant way and the light of the Holy Father will shine down upon you.'

'Thank you.'

'My blessings and, as you see, the rain has gone and diminished and we are bringing you back your fair weather.'

'Thank you.'

'My blessings upon you and the Holy Father shines his light upon you both and holds you as his dear, dear children and you are very loved and very embraced and very awaited in our space. Goodbye my dear ones.'

TIME TO GO FORWARD AND
ENJOY BEING FREE

Kuthumi

'It's so wonderful to see you both again as the two wonderful lights that I mentioned before. Don't be sad, as this is supposed to be one of the happiest times of your life and, by saying this, I know how hard you are both working trying to go up to that other dimension but, dear ones, the time will come and just be yourself as you always have been and enjoy the wonderful energy of the holy ones that surround you at all times. Yes, dear Mary?'

'We felt it was you coming in because we were laughing and being very joyful. I thank you for your wonderful presence. We just wondered because both of us went through a rather, well, trying experience this weekend, if you could tell us what went on for both of us during the weekend?'

'Yes, indeed, but don't be sad by this. This will be something that your friend will understand probably better than you Mary, but it's like a little bird that got out of its nest and is ready to fly and he pulls his wings and he exercises and he is ready to fly but then, yet, it has a little fear to get out of the nest because it might fall and see how steep it is, so the father and the mother just push it along and by doing this it falls and it flies: the fear is over for that little bird. That's exactly what went on this weekend with you both. It's a time to go forward

160

and the Holy Father came up with the wonderful angels and surrounded you with that wonderful energy that you all had but then, yet, you said to yourselves: "I haven't fallen out of that nest yet, I am not ready for that flight yet". So he came down and he pushed you and you both fell because you both didn't expect it to be that way.

You thought you would just lift off your body and get up to that wonderful energy that's out there but, dear ones, you have to make that first step and by making that first step is to be free completely. What I mean by completely is let nothing hold you back. Yes, that was a bad experience but there will be a better one for you if you just set up your hearts and say: "Dear Father, I am ready for you; I have been ready for you since the day I was born". Yes, lift up your souls completely and your bodies should be light like that feather and you will fly just like you see a star that's moving from one place to another, a shining star: you will be beamed up that fast just like that. So, I am saying to you: don't worry; carry on with whatever you are doing and be more yourself; don't work so hard for that goal that you are trying to reach – it will come automatically to you. As I can see it, the aggravation – the madness if you like to call it – and they told me, the wonderful energy told me I am ready; this will be the time. "What have I done?" You haven't done anything wrong. The time will come whenever you are and they are ready for you. So, it's not your fault, this is just a trial if you like to call it, but the real thing will happen and then you will be very surprised at what will be. So, please, carry on the wonderful work that you are all doing.'

'Thank you St Francis. If we lighten up in our hearts, will that help a great deal?'

'The same way you came to this wonderful chapel: try to leave the same way you came in – probably even a little bit lighter and shine that light around your dear ones – friends and enemies – and don't be afraid to speak up saying that you are a Light Being and speak up on their behalf, on your behalf but

161

not to overrate yourself, if you know what I am trying to say, not to be put on the spot but encourage them – those that need to be encouraged – in a nice manner, just like that wonderful little bird that tried to push that little bird to fly and you, Mary, you are doing a great job at the moment – please carry on.'

'Thank you Kuthumi. I imagine that there would be this doorframe in light blue shimmering colours and that I would wake up and say, "Oh good, there's the door and I shall walk through", but I didn't see any door, at least not that I remember.'

'As I said before, it will be different for each individual: you all have your own ascension path. Some of you will fall asleep, you might think you are dreaming and you will awaken out there and then you will come back on your own. That will be something that I would be very proud to talk to you about eventually. And some others – they can be just walking down the road, their bodies will still be there and they will be uplifted. When the time comes, he will say: "This is your time and we are ready for you". He will just pick you up wherever you are so don't be afraid going to bed and going to sleep, carry on your duties and when the time comes – wherever you are – you will be uplifted and no one except you and your wonderful Guides will know where you are going.'

'Well, my friend saw a vision of himself walking along the hallway in the house and he felt himself falling and he saw me catch him. Was that significant of something?'

'Yes indeed, dear one. As I have mentioned, this little bird fell out of its nest and thought he couldn't fly so automatically he fell down and there were you as the mother as always and picked him up and just put him back where he was supposed to be, in his nest. I thank you.'

'I thank you. This is beautiful; it gives me such a feeling of

162

lightness and not being so responsible and having to do this and having to do that. I think I needed to hear you in order to lighten up.'

'As the Light Beings that you are, see what's inside the flame of a candle; you can put your hand through it, it might feel warm and if you are fast enough you won't feel anything. Then, yet, the power that is there, the energy that's there is remarkable as human beings are. The energy is there, your Light Spirits are there, so you are that burning flame at all time, but imagine a little candle: how does it light up a whole room and the people around it? You as a Light Being do exactly the same thing but without being noticeable. In fact, some people sometimes turn you on and turn you off, if you wish to call it that way. When you are there as a Light Being, you always shine and that's why we call upon you to light up those around you, even those that are far away from you, a nice word that's cheerful – it will lighten them up. Think of that as a candle in their room – just light up their whole life. We are Light Beings dear one so that's one of the points that I would like to bring up to you and you will feel yourself proud and honoured but don't take that as a present. Say: "Dear Father, I am doing what you asked me to do and I hope that you will give me more and more energy and light me up a little bit brighter that I can light even more and more of the dark world." Thanks dear one.'

'May I ask two more questions?'

'Yes, dear one.'

'We wanted to know if there was anything we could have done that would have been better in order to cooperate with the Guides and the Light Beings who were around us this weekend?'

'You were doing very well and I have to congratulate you on that part. That's what they will love to see as you really

163

light up: being happy and enjoying every step of the way and then it came to the following day and they saw you so down again. They said: "What happened to that candle, that wonderful light: did we blow it out?", and then, dear one, that candle, eventually, the energy was so high and then it just came back down – where the wax is kept – it went pretty well almost blank, but they tried to remove that wax from you and that's why they are there for you. They would like to see you at all times being that wonderful candle and just shining. The more you shine, the happier you will be and let no one take that away from you.'

'I think the obligation of writing all of those Christmas cards did pull me down, but when it's finished I won't do any more. St Francis, I think there is one last question here. Will something happen before Christmas or are we not understanding the process, or is it God's decision when we will be taken?'

'Dear ones, I cannot answer this very important question for you – it's up to each individual. Whenever you feel free and when He knows you are completely ready and free of burdens He will come down and uplift you in his own way, but don't rush yourself, don't work yourself up to a point that you feel that you have been let down somehow: He doesn't let anyone down; He loves each individual and if He could have taken you on Saturday He would have, but your time was not up yet, and they are not ready for you at the moment. Whenever they are ready, they will come down with bright lights and they will take you to that other realm, much the same way as you will accept them in your own heart.'

'Is there another way that I will feel them when they are present like we did this weekend?'

'You will not only feel them, you will be able to see them more clearly and yes, dear one, carry on that wonderful conversation as they try to light you up and get yourself ready for that wonderful moment. You will know when you are ready.'

'Thank you. You have blessed me this day. I think my disappointment came from waking up the next morning and finding it was all the same, but I won't do that again.'

'I thank you for understanding and by understanding your-self, you actually admitted it, that was your own light. You want to be ready so much for that, that you were willing to take that giant step and, of course, I can see the dark spot coming out of you when you woke up that morning. But, dear one, if you had just woken up the same way you fell asleep, you would have been a lot lighter and a lot happier.'

'Is there anything for my friend, St Francis?'

'Tell him not to be so hard on himself. He is good at not judging others but he tries to judge himself. It's not very good for him to do that at this particular time. Let him be free and the wonderful advice he gives to others and the energy – tell him: "we are not here to judge – not even ourselves – so please go as you always have, encourage the others, and at the same time you have to encourage yourself and be ready", because at the moment, yes, he has some similarity to you: "This was meant to happen and it did not happen: what did I do wrong?". You are not doing anything wrong, but just don't judge yourself, let yourself be and, as I said before, wake up in that wonderful light and just feel the love and the energy that they all have to offer you. You will feel a lot better inside and out and you shall shine brighter and brighter around those that you meet and talk to. I thank you.'

'Thank you. God bless you for your beautiful words and the encouragement you are giving to these little birds that aren't quite ready yet. Thank you Kuthumi.'

'These blessings are amongst us all. I thank you for coming here in such truthful meaning; that I can send my love to all of you and for you to carry on the wonderful things that you are all doing. I thank you and may our Holy Father always shine the wonderful light and may your surprise come early so you don't have to be in so much agony as a child cannot wait to open that little box that he receives for Christmas to see what's inside. Dear ones, you are becoming like that little child – be patient and be surprised at what's inside that little box. I thank you both.'

* * *

'I say good evening to you. For such a beautiful evening is something to behold. Can you look out there my dears and see the colour of the sky, the pink shade of the clouds? Can you see the loveliness of the trees, the water, the reflections upon it, how life is treating you my dears? My name is Quan Yin and I come to you from the desert so, for me, it is very refreshing to see this environment and to know that you, too, are here, my dear, dear ones. Though it has not seemed I was present for you very often, I have followed you everywhere and I have embraced you at night and I have reassured you when you got depressed, picked you up when you have fallen and put you straight upon your paths again, and I hear your hearts are hurting, you are longing for something you know is very close and very near and something you can attain to and you will. It is not to be discouraging and not to be thought that it is out of your reach because you cannot touch it; for, my dears, it is one thing in your lifetime that you can desire but it cannot be visualised, it cannot be touched, it cannot be felt nor can you ring the shopping channel and ask them to please send it to your home. Now we laugh and we keep it light because it must be, my dears, in that love and laughter and the light and happiness that the Holy Father sends down to us there is no sadness, there is no failure, there is no right way or wrong way nor punishing yourselves because you didn't get the message properly and you tried very hard and you applied yourselves

166

but nothing happened, no result came out and you are questioning, you are questioning yourselves, your own abilities.

You are questioning the Guides who are coming in and the very process which is the one thing which we want you to love and yearn for and have it become, not just a goal that you attain to, but something alive and real, something that you are touching when you are touching a tree – embrace it and say: "I am embracing enlightenment, I am embracing ascension", and when you are walking on the grass say: "Grass, I know you are leading me on that path to ascension and I might come around the bend and there it is and, oh birds, you are talking to me now but aren't you giving me messages about my ascension and telling me that it's not far away?". Encourage yourselves, my dears. Talk to yourselves, let the Spirit of the land, the Spirit of the water come forth; talk to the stars when you are looking at them at night and say: "Beautiful stars I see you twinkling at me; you may be a spaceship, I do not know, but I know that I want to be close to you and I know I will be because you are representing to me that visual point that I am reaching out for which is my spiritual path", and don't be discouraged if it hasn't come and if it isn't the way you had imagined it all in a box and tied up with pretty paper and a ribbon and looking very festive because it's something you could put under the Christmas tree and say: "This has been an achievement and I have something to show for it".

We don't need that and I don't think you do. If you look deep into your heart, can you hear my words? They are calming, they are reassuring, they are coming to you as a mother would come who is wise and has been through it before and has known this kind of suffering that you are speaking of. I do want to hear your questions after this, but I know, as well, that I tried so hard myself because all the men could do it and I was told that because I was a woman I would never attain to enlightenment and I had best give up and ask to be re-born as a child, an infant boy who could certainly attain to enlightenment – even as a youngster – but that it was not proper for a woman to want this because there was a difference and women did not have the same attributes as men. But I

167

knew in my heart – hear me – I knew in my heart that I was right.

Do you see, all these people were giving me messages not realising that they were putting me down; they thought they were wise, that they had the knowledge that I did not, they were speaking to me as the wise ones; the ancient texts were available to them, they had read all about it, they knew it, they had lived it in lifetimes and I was only a woman, and, according to them, I was supposed to be a man, but they could not deny my devotion nor my regularity when I showed up and I was always there asking for more: give me penitence, give me poverty, give me humility, give me whatever you need to, but I need to experience these because I know, too, that I can transverse that veil, I can break through it as much as anyone because my heart is there and it is longing for me to reach that space. I also knew I had Guides around me. They were there encouraging me, they were urging me on and I, too, felt disciplined in the sense that I must respond quickly, I must not be neglectful or, my goodness, if I do miss one prayer one night or say it wrong or not move my rosary beads appropriately I will not succeed because these men are telling me I cannot succeed. I am not saying that the guidance you have received up to the present is not the right guidance, I am saying that it must be something you feel and that you long for and that you pray to the Holy Father that it will come because you know it is wonderful and you know that everything around you is telling you this is your path and they are leading you, they are guiding you. At night the Guides are wonderful and they are loving and Mary has a wonderful Guide who has feathers and she can cuddle up under him and find even a pocket within his wings and go out to the universe and explore. It doesn't mean that that wonderful Guide is going to take her to the place she wants to be but it's a comforting place to be in and she loves it and she's thanking the Guide and she's grateful – there's nothing more to it than that.

We ask you to pray for the Holy Father, pray to him like a brother – He is there, He is listening. You are very special beings. I need to pause here to tell you that, my dears, that you are loved because you are here to encourage one another and we know of the disappointments: you've tried to teach classes, you have tried to bring in individuals to this wonderful island and they acknowledge it is wonderful and then they go on with their lives as if to say: "Well, that was interesting but now I have something more interesting to do", and they drop it but you have not my precious ones. May I reiterate this, may I underline it, underscore it, put it in neon signs: you have not been abandoned because you never gave up on God – have you not my dears?'

'Thank you. That is very comforting. I feel a lot better right now. I have a question for you, I hope you don't mind. Is it true that Mary's problem is impatience, expectation and having to deal with pain and being tired? Please help us explain that.'

'I believe, my dears, this is if you have to put it in medical or therapy terms, it could have labels such as expectations, intolerance, impatience – I have heard those words from many people of your sort who are also longing for ascension because I am out there for many, as you can imagine and I also have to thank you for providing me the space to interact with beings who reach out to me wherever they may be on this planet, but I have a home to return to and it is a beautiful space.
I am saying to you, my dears, all those words may be applied and they have been applied to people who have tortured themselves, that they have not done it right: I say to you, my dears, look into your hearts and your heart longings. It's not a question of putting a label on it now. Pain may certainly be acknowledged, and if it is the will of the Holy Father we know you will accept it, but love yourselves even if it means taking your arms and putting them around yourselves and saying: "I love this body, I love everything: the attributes that the Holy Father has given me, I love my process, I love where I am and I know that all my needs will be met and taken care of. I am not forgotten and I know that and all the Guides that are surrounding me are witness to the fact that I love them

and I welcome them and acknowledge them and I am doing the very best that I can."

I want no blame to come from my mouth ever to say you have not done it right, my dears – you are doing everything and more. Perhaps if there is one thing I could say to you: you are doing too much. It's all so simple if you just simply love the process, love where you are, touch the tree and thank it for bringing you to enlightenment, touch the miracle of the sunset and say: "Thank you sunset for reminding me of my enlightenment". Bring it into your every day vocabulary; thank the lizards, thank the ants, the biggest creatures and the smallest creatures for bringing you to this space for they are all part of your universe and as you acknowledge them and thank them for they are truly God's creatures. You are also thanking the creator who is making this illumination, this electrification, this incredible opportunity to serve, whatever you wish to call it. He is making it possible, my dears, and by your loving every bit of your life, every instant of it, every morsel of food you eat, every smile you get from your child and as you hold their face tell them how precious they are, that's all that the Father is asking for you to do – it's nothing more. Love those spaces, love yourselves, love the precious beings, the precious situations that are coming to you – even if they are testing you and trying your patience especially at Christmas time.'

'Thank you. It seems to us that this process is like giving birth. Is that true?'

'A likely similarity. I did go through those feelings myself when I first went through my own emancipation. It is painful and it is not a punishment for you – everyone who is going through it and doing it properly will feel the pain. It is pain because it is separating you from the third dimension which is heavy, it is glue-like, it's like stepping into quicksand. It wants to envelop you and pull you down and you are saying "No" to it. You are lighter than it, you are separating yourself from a dynamo of energy, of volatility, of activity, of denseness and you are saying: "I choose this path", and, as you separate,

170

naturally there is tension in this space and all of its beings that interact within it do not want to let you go, they want you as part of them because you are bringing in light and you are bringing in energy and activating spaces and they say, "Good, that makes more praise for us to feed on". Can you see it is not a healthy environment that you are in right now, in fact it is looked upon in the universe as one of the darkest and the most devilish places that exists in the universe. Do not give it attention, my dears. All I am saying is the more attention you give to it, the more pain there will be from this releasing. Just love everything that is happening, if it means that you look at your pain and say: "I do feel like I am giving birth but I know it will end and I know that it is a wonderful thing and I am happy for it, I bless it, I love it and just touch your body where it's hurting and just say: "Heavenly Father, help me release the pain", just bring it up your legs or across your stomachs or over your heads; your hands are like magic and I will see to it that the energy that you have in your hands will release it and say: "Dear Heavenly Father, I feel the tension in my head as if I have a fever: would you release it?". Take your hands up and just see the Heavenly Father coming down in love and light and taking it away.'

'That's beautiful. I think I'll try that. Is it wise for us to know where we are going at night; particularly myself?'

'You are very blessed for your Guides have felt that you did not need this pain. We're not saying that Mary has had to suffer because of pain but she is particularly sensitive to this type of environment and energy and that is why she picks up on the pain because there is a pulling that is going on for her not to leave but, for you, if you sail off like you are a balloon and you are escaping out into the universe and you don't know where, then know that you are blessed, my dear. It is not to trouble yourself with it but we do ask that you be there punctually and you make it a long night for those long nights are wondrous. From our side we marvel, we welcome you, we cheer you on and say: "Good, you're here," and you shall be making that difference when you go back with all the things that you are going to do when you return. So, do you see, there is hardly enough time; we want more of you. You wonder if you are doing the wrong thing – believe me it is more right than right can be.'

'Thank you. I think you have answered all of our questions. One more question. You moved and allowed us to see you when we were meditating in your room. Will that happen again?'

'You can see me at any time, my dears, you have that faculty and it would be nice if you would visualise me before you go to sleep. Ask for my arms to embrace you, to uplift you, to take you to that safe space whereby your transition may go smoothly. I am always there for you, my dears, though you have not always called upon me and I did not want you to feel that it was an obligation for you have many Guides and many followers clambering to be around you and there is a selection that is happening – not that some Guides are not good for you and that they are being removed – that is not the case but as your energy is evolving, you are naturally attracting certain Guides that have always been there for you – not just in this lifetime, but in many lifetimes. Can you see yourselves spiralling up and as you spiral up, the ones who might have dealt with, say, those who are starting to channel or who are starting their process, will be released to go and work with the others who are, perhaps, more needy at that stage. You see, you do not require that much attention in that respect. What you are needing is uplifting and more opening and more awareness as to who you are and that timing is very important right now so that when you do go across that veil and through to your enlightenment, that at a certain precise time these messages will be decoded and released to your cognizant mind. They are there in pockets, if you will but you do not know of them now. When they are needed, then they will be released. So, at that time, your expansion will be magnificent. I cannot describe it – like a quasar exploding and we are going

172

to see someone who believed himself to be a limited being becoming an expanded master. We rejoice for that and do not be impatient my dear. If I have told you, as others have said, it will happen before Christmas will you trust me?'

'Indeed. One question: when is Christmas?'

'Very wise, from an old priest who has known that date was chosen and was not the actual birth of the infant Jesus. It was to align itself with the winter solstice and, also, the rituals from the northern civilisations: the ones who celebrated with the Christmas tree and had their time of Yuletide being aligned with the longest days of the year and the darkest moments when they were needing that light. So, all this has changed and evolved. If I give you the date of the 5th January my dear, that would be more appropriate but when I say before Christmas, I do mean your Christmas celebration on planet Earth. For the most part, the Christian world would celebrate it on the 25th December and that is the date we are speaking of.'

'Thank you. I think that's it and I thank you for being here with us.'

'Try to visualise the light that is around me my dear as you are going to sleep. Can you see my head-dress? You do see it above my head do you not? It is rather like a crown intermixed with the hair that is tied back. You also see my long earlobes. You visualise my eyes, but will you notice my heart because my heart chakra is there within it. My heart, my third eye and my crown chakra: those are the three points I want you to focus on and, as you do, you will begin to see a colour in my aura and as you pick up that colour, you might pick out another one that is blended with it but is also distinct from it and then you might see rays coming out of it. These are very beneficial for you my dears and if you can visualise those rays, that light, my aura would extend up about as high as this ceiling in the chapel and if you can picture all of it, then you are in a very sacred energy and nothing will disturb you, no pain will come in to you and your aura will enlarge as much as mine. So, by symbiosis, you will take on my characteristics and my process, for your faithfulness, for your love and for being the disciples you have been, I wish to acknowledge you. You have always come to us and you have always asked for our help. I am giving you this additional help to put you at peace now so that your nights may be restful and you may awaken in the arms of your beloved Father.'

'Thank you.'

'Blessings upon you my dears and in the light and love of the Holy Father and the sanctity of his being and the acknowledgement that he is giving you images of who you are and what magnificence awaits you! I praise you and honour you and ask that these blessings be bestowed – not just upon you – but upon all those who adhere to the doctrines so faithfully and so religiously. I bid you adieu and I shall be with you this evening.'

'I am looking forward to it.'

'Amen.'

* * *

'We greet you and welcome you.'

'Is this Kuthumi?'

'Yes indeed.'

'Thank you for coming Kuthumi. I came in this morning earlier; I just felt like I wanted to bow before your picture. I am not sure if it was your voice telling me not to be bowing in front of the cross. Did I make a mistake?'

'No, dear one. You should not ever believe a feeling was a

174

mistake, the feeling that you came in with, and that intention is good enough for all of us.'

'I have a problem that has to do with drugs. It seems like the papers are dealing with it; the news is very bad about the children here being not just exposed to drugs, but selling them – it's surrounding me somehow. Is there something that my friend and I could do or is this just a "wait and see" process, is there an idea you have because I know he is worried his children are also in danger?'

'That's a wonderful point you bring up. Drugs make innocent little ones do evil things: it turns them against our Holy Father. They don't know what's causing it, but we do. Yes, both of you can do something about that in the future but, at the moment, I don't see anything but just pray for them and ask, when you see someone coming to you for help – Heavenly Father help me with this "lost soul". Then get inside them: why have they gone beyond the straight road that they used to be following so clearly and so cleverly; that road they have taken is wonderful. There are so many excuses that they come up with: taking drugs, drinking – it's all an excuse. It's to fulfil something missing, someone that they don't have in themselves. They feel like a person who is hungry: they have to eat to survive. That is a hunger that is missing inside, a true spiritual longing. So they are hungry for drugs, but if that could be fulfilled with something else, for some of them it might be too late, but some others you can wake up and say that there are other ways it can be done without that, by not cutting them completely from whatever they are doing – because their bodies are so used to this, but cut them off gradually; bring them down to nothing eventually and the less that they take the better they will eat, the more proud they will be of themselves. The younger ones will be easier to deal with than the older ones. The older ones have set their goals. For some the wound is so deep that it is too late for them to drop whatever they are doing to heal themselves. You can suggest, you can do your best but they will always be hungry for it, they will always have that urge that they have to have it. Until they have it, they cannot go in the public areas because they feel that they are not themselves, they are not sure: all that comes into them and until they take this, as I call it "poison", they do not feel that they can go out in public.

Yes, channelling: it's very good for those that believe, but, others would not believe in that. Hypnotic suggestion is another good way to stop them for a couple of days but then again, after they feel that emptiness, they are going to crave whatever they should not have and it's immediate gratification. So, you get a balance, you get the one that has been broken since he was a child and you have the ones that actually reached the peak and said: "I can't go any higher now", so they end up drinking, smoking because they are at that level where there is nothing left to challenge any more; they have challenged everything – they are at the top. Those who are at the top are going to be the hardest ones to convince that there is still something else they can do and even if they don't have to they can go to school to higher levels of education, to become lawyers or to obtain any other degree that they wish to achieve. They have to be kept occupied all the time and the more time that they find for themselves, they start sitting back and thinking and then they go back to their bad environment again. So, the busier you keep these people, the less time they will have to think and fall back into their old habits. So how can one keep them always occupied? It's not a very easy task, dear one, but if you can get them involved in a project – whatever project it will be – even if it's creating a game or creating some new talent, be out there to help the community – get them involved in everyday life and the more involved they are, with the right community, of course, the better they will feel about themselves. They will feel proud. These are the ones that are up there and that say they have done it all, they don't have anything else to do; these are the ones that need to do charity work, if you wish to call it that, but get them involved with the right society and whatever you do with this society, make sure they are not against blacks or whites, against religion or anything of that sort. Make sure they are in the right environment. Then again, where are you going to find this kind of environment to give to them? So, it comes to the bottom of the pit, you fulfil their hearts the same way as I have just explained and explain that to them, put the ideas out to them and make them work with it and practice it; make them feel that their Higher Self loves them – even if they are at the top and they have reached their goal. For some who don't believe in God, try and let them work spiritually if they wish to and let them work on their own. Maybe a new creation with a group can be challenging to one another. Say: "Let's see who's going to create the best idea for this project, and let's go and see who's going to last the longest without the need for the medicine that they are taking" and see where they go from there. Every day will be a bigger and better step for them if they establish themselves under their own steam and, yes, let them scream out if they have to, let the anger come out of them – that's what they feel.

At the same time show them, if you have one, a film on alcoholism: that will put a picture in front of their faces because that is something they have forgotten. They will see how they were then and are now and there are some good films on alcohol abuse, drugs abuse. Show them a film and bring them back to the beginning of what they were and see how wonderful they were and where are they now, where the light has taken from them: some of them with AIDS, some of them have cancer and they are just popping off unnecessarily. I hope that will be a start for you.'

'Would it be something we could do here on the island or is that too dangerous?'

'It could be done with a handful of people and then spread it out slowly towards those communities that need it the most and eventually, yes, dear ones, think of schools where they will be taught. Eventually, I would wish that they start to teach this in kindergarten exactly what alcohol does to them and start it from there by putting them in the right environment. Of course a lot of these wonderful children say: "My mummy and daddy: they are taking that stuff too". So they look up to their parents as Guides and then it is up to the teacher to explain to them. Don't find an excuse for the children. The pressure that the parents are under today – they use that to hide like you play hide and go seek – they are doing that to themselves and that is very, very dangerous, dear ones, so please don't get upset with them but go home and say: "Mummy and Daddy, I love you the way you are, please leave that stuff alone so you can watch my grandchildren". If they can get that and hear what these big hearts are saying, the parents will understand and maybe, slowly and eventually they will give it up and the child will look up to them and say: "Thank you and you have made this a wonderful world to be in".'

'Oh, dear Kuthumi, it's overwhelming. I want to do it all and you make it sound so easy. I just pray for the courage to start somewhere and, with your proper guidance, I know we can do it.'

'I thank you for asking a very important question and I know you will all come up with a solution.'

'And Kuthumi, is that big crystal that is coming to the Isle making a big shift in the energy?'

'It will indeed but it takes humans like you to fulfil that little love and make it grow and expand and the more love it gets the more it will expand into the universe and, eventually, yes, but put those wonderful ideas of yours and thoughts with your love and send it out there and, as I say, a wonderful prayer that will change the negative energy that surrounds those beings who are trapped in the land and make that a freeing of their energy what you are about to do. That will make things a lot easier for you and for all who come to work and study here.'

'Thank you Kuthumi and blessings and my love. We feel

178

very protected and very looked after with your guidance. Thank you.'

'It's always an honour to be here with wonderful Spirits, shining up with your wonderful light and at this moment I will just ask the Holy One to embrace you all with love and carry you throughout this miserable and nasty transformation that is occurring in the universe, that it will turn brighter and brighter and you will all wake up.'

BE CHEERFUL AND LOVE
YOURSELVES AT ALL TIMES

Kuthumi

'I am delighted you have taken some time to come out to this wonderful chapel. I thank you; both of you. Yes, dear Mary?'

'We feel very much at home here. You are Kuthumi are you not?'

'Yes.'

'Well, Merry Christmas Kuthumi. It seems like there are so many celebrations but it's not really the celebration that I am praying for. I want to be more with our spiritual friends and I hope it will happen soon.'

'Yes. I do feel your disappointment with this at the present but, dear ones, celebrate just like you would in a very nice, happy atmosphere and be free at all times and do not let any hesitation bother you; just be yourself, carry on with what you are doing and maybe you will be surprised by what will happen. Don't wake up in the morning disappointed – be proud that you still have your wonderful Guides around you and that you still see the beautiful world around you and love everything that surrounds you and thank the Holy One for your

180

being there, even if you haven't gone for your journey but it will happen to you so please, I beg you, be cheerful and love yourself at all times and do not be disappointed. There is nothing that you are doing wrong to hold you here. You are doing everything that is possible and everything is getting ready for the "right time", shall I call it. So, dear one, just thank the Holy One for everything that is around you and be loved and love everything that is around you.'

'I feel your love Kuthumi and it touches me very deeply and I thank you because I see the infinite wisdom in allowing my friend and myself to still be here because it is such a busy time of the year and many people depend upon us and need that special attention so it was highest wisdom I am sure.'

'Thank you for your understanding.'

'May I ask if it is true that at night I am working in the astral belt: somehow I have that feeling? Is that a misconception?'

'Not working in the astral belt, but they are working with you. How can I explain this for you to understand. There is a road between here and space and you are, in other words, going for your horseriding lesson and you are riding that wonderful horse on this wonderful road and, of course, yes, it doesn't feel like you are advancing; but every day you get a little bit further and further on this wonderful horse and then you know your way up and then you get to this distance and then you turn around and come back to your natural body and every day you are doing that, you are going up a little bit further and further and then you will know that road very well and then you just come right back. And you are doing this slowly until one day you will get to the top and then you will know your way up and down so easily that you can just blink your eyes and you will be there; just take a deep breath and you will be back.

This is the progress that is going on through you at the

moment. Yes dear one, this pain, this agony, that pushing and fighting to get up there; that's wonderful and we love you for that but, at the same time, be patient and just love everything that they are doing for you and you are doing for them and just embrace those little angels that surround you at all times and love them the way you have been doing so far and they will sing up in Heaven with you one day. So please, just be loved – whatever you are doing is correct and I pray for you that everything will happen in God's will at the right time.'

'And I bless you Kuthumi for explaining it to me; it makes it easier if I understand it so that I won't be judging myself and say I've done something wrong when it hurts in the morning. My friend and I were wondering why he is able to watch TV and I am not. Is there a reason?'

'Yes, dear one. You are very, very fragile to everything as our dear ones have told you before, you are so wonderful that your energy is almost like the inside of a flower, the bees go in there and take that wonderful juice, to suck it out and make honey out of it but, in this case, it is not bees that are coming for your energy, this negative energy that comes in there and they take that wonderful energy that you do have and that's one of the reasons we do not recommend you watch TV because you are open. Even if you see a good show; if there is a commercial that comes in with any bad vibration, you will pick that up automatically – you are very sensible that way not to watch the TV. So, please dear one, this not only goes for TV; this also goes for theatres, movies and places that you walk along; you do pick this up because you are very, very wonderful indeed and they see this coming to you and even though you don't realise it, you open up to them, you still love them just like you love anyone else. That is wonderful of you but, at the same time, we do not want you to suffer the way you have been suffering and we would advise you please just let the light that you have given to so many to come and protect yourself and say: "Dear Holy Father, this is not my doing, so please, if they are not welcome with me, could you please

182

remove them from me and put them in the bright light that they will never return to the dark again". That's one of the main reasons I do not recommend you to watch TV dear one and, at the same time, as you know, you have other things that you wish to do than just sit watching your TV.'

'Thank you Kuthumi. No, I don't really want to watch TV anymore. My friend was asking why doesn't he pick up the astral entities like I do?'

'As a Light Being the way he is, he can change almost like a split personality and he could be in line with us at all times and then he can put a veil in front of him and he can see right through that veil; it's almost like a shield and nothing can come towards him. He can walk freely wherever he goes and that, if you like to call "a shell", that he carries with him, he doesn't even have to worry about it, it's a gift that he has received many, many years ago and he does use it. It's wonderful that he can do this without any negative energy coming through to him and he is very, very fortunate that he can do those sorts of things.'

'Will he be able to teach this at some point?'

'If necessary, yes. He does have that knowledge.'

'Perhaps when he comes back as a master he will be.'

'It's coming soon and he will know. So, if he has to, he will.'

'I haven't much else to ask you Kuthumi but I wanted to know if there was something else I could do to support the Arcturians around me? I feel them: they're gentle, they're loving, they're caring and I just want to know if they are needing something that I am not picking up on?'

'As I said a few minutes ago, dear one, just love them and

183

send your love to them and sing with them if you can and put on some good music – the one that is your favourite – and they will dance with you and be happy with you. That's one of the wonderful things about being a Light Being as you are. You are never alone. They say Christmas time is supposed to be a family time but what more of a family can you have than those that love you by the Light, by the heart without any strings attached. They come to you, dear one, with love and they are always around you. Any time you feel lonely, just call upon them and they will be with you, so be happy with that. Yes, dear one, play some cheerful music with them, dance if you wish to and just be happy with that. They want to see you happy and they are guiding you and they are there for you. I beg you dear one, have fun with them.'

'They're so loving and light and wonderful and I know how brilliant they are. I feel it must be very dense and difficult for them to be here.'

'If you just knew and once you get up there, you will do exactly the same thing once you find that there are human beings on Earth like you are; you will be doing exactly the same thing.'

'Have I lived on Arcturus before so I understand them?'

'Yes, dear one, and they are cousins to you and they are here to help you. You will be amazed at the discovery of this. I beg you to go there and have fun with them and you will communicate with them very clearly the way you have been doing but with more eyesight than just the energy. So, please, have fun and just watch them: those little wonderful bright lights shining and flapping their wings with you and I will not say any more.'

'I love you Kuthumi and I pray that we may honour you because you have done so much to support us and uplift us and I want you to be proud of us someday.'

184

'I am very proud of you and the others that are doing this wonderful work and anything that I do, dear one, is the love of our Holy Father that asks me to be here with you and guide you to the right "road", if you like to call it, and maybe one day we can all embrace together as brothers and sisters instead of just feeling the energy that I bring down to you and to receive the wonderful energy I am receiving from you. I beg you to go and have a wonderful time and, please, do not hesitate to call on my name any time you wish to and the ones around you. We beg you to cheer up and be the wonderful Light Beings that we see above from Heaven and up in space at all times. So, please, be that wonderful being, be that wonderful light and just shine brighter and brighter. As I have explained, the brighter the light that shines, the lighter you will become and the easier it will be for you to come and meet us one day. I beg you to have a great time and may I go in peace and leave you in bright light as our Holy Father commands me to do dear one. Amen.'

FILLING ONE'S SELF WITH THE GOLDEN LIGHT

Kuthumi

'When Jesus Sananda knew that he was to be crucified, he used to go up into the mountains depressed, meditating, asking for guidance, for the Holy One to come and help him. You are going through a similar progression. Do not be afraid – be thankful. It is the most wonderful thing that a human being can receive so anytime that you feel like that again, yes, take a walk, pray out loud or play your favourite music and sing along with it; be cheerful and happy and then come back to your regular exercises the way you were taught. It will happen to you – I'm not going to tell you the exact date and the time because you should not know that. It should come as a surprise dear one and I want you to feel it that way and that way you will just carry on doing your exercises and it will happen to you automatically before your eyes. So dear one, do not be sad – be cheerful. As tears drop out of the human's eyes so also blood flows down to our hearts. Feel the love that we carry and give to you. So yes, dear one, if I can help you any further please?'

'Thank you. I ask this because knowing what I am going through I would like to be able to assist others when they come to that point and I thank you for it. I do believe it was a breakthrough for me to admit that I was tired, that I had been working too hard, that I was hurting and I felt no validation and I think that was what was hurting most. Is that correct?'

'Indeed, but when you feel doubt, think about the wonders that you have done for others. You see them coming to you for assistance, for help. Even though you do not realise how much you are helping them, every day you are doing something for someone else. Think of that; see how important you are on planet Earth and spiritually. I am not just saying that to upgrade you; I am just saying that because you are a very wonderful being and I see a wonderful light shining above you every day – even on the darkest night I can still see it. It is very wonderful to see beings like that that have that sole bright light almost like the Sun shining down, reflecting into the water and reflecting to your face and feeling warm and healthy. You have that energy in you and as long as you carry it with you, use it for your own self; just bring up your Higher Self and say: "Dear Father, I am your lovely daughter; I love you dear one; please take care of me and guide me how I can fulfil my needs". He will give you that answer; he will fulfil every need that you desire. Please, dear one, be happy. It's so easy to say, "Be happy? How can I be happy if I don't feel it"? You can make a direct turn like a whirlpool, you can either go down or up. When that whirlpool is going down, you are sinking and that is the time of depression. Well you too can just turn around and go back up by blowing that energy around your body; fill yourself with that wonderful energy of Golden Light they will bring to you and say: "Dear one, I thank you for the wonderful help and the wonderful angels you have surrounded me with", and see those angels just carrying you up further and further to the dimension you have been waiting for.'

'I only say that, for me, the most difficult part is when my body hurts and I did believe that I was back with pneumonia and having to take antibiotics. I wish to be able to help people in those circumstances. Is there anything further I can do for others as you are doing for me?'

'You will be able to do these exact same exercises with them and show how easily they can be done. Pain should not come to the bodies that are so light and ready to take off in the flash of light. The pain that you receive is years and years of building up so release that pain but keep releasing in your own time as you feel the pain and fulfil yourself with that wonderful Golden Light that you always know is right underneath your heart. If you can do that, the pain will not come back to that particular spot and just keep going further and further and fulfil again those little dark spots with that wonderful Golden Light that you receive and we know is love. Yes, love yourself; it's very, very important that you do love yourself indeed and not for one moment doubt yourself. When you start doubting yourself you begin to get negative energy back to those wonderful lights that you fulfil so much with love.'

'I thank you and I have no more questions. You have filled me with love and I am blessed.'

'And this dear one, please, I beg you, go out and preach to those who are in the same levitation as you are. I may go now and at any time, you can call up our dear ones and we will be here to assist you. Amen.'

188

BEING RE-ALIGNED BY THE MASTERS

Melchisedeck

'I am Melchisedeck. I am Mary's mentor. Most of her programming is decided by the Wise Ones in consultation with myself and Master Metitron. We do sometimes have an assembly of Guides that we work with and you, as well, we align you to similar energies. You may have wondered at some time how you two are so perfectly aligned in being the perfect masculine energy and the perfect feminine energy to complement one another. It is because there is a homogeneity, a harmony, that is a result of your work together. There is love and excitement and commitment on your behalf, both of you, so that when you work together there is a stimulating process; you come together with your own burdens or worries or excitement but it multiplies as you are together with the effect of our work around you. Imagine yourselves in a bubble whereby the charge is given to the bubble and you are within it. We are not saying we are electrocuting you within this bubble, it is more stimulating; it is working on your nerve fibres; it is working on your intelligence, on your capacity to retain knowledge that we are giving you at night; it is working on your sensitivity, on opening your heart chakras, on stimulating all of your chakra systems so that you are becoming more alive than almost any of the humans walking on this Earth.

You may marvel sometimes at how it is that you complement one another when one is needing support: the other one is

189

up and when it is the reverse, you are there to help one another in perfect synchronicity; it is flowing so that we can almost give knowledge to one and have the other receive it. Can you see it light a figure eight, moving and spiralling up and around and, as you do that, you are coming in contact with one another, stimulating one another, reaching out, circling round, coming back with that knowledge? Do you feel this as I describe it?'

'Yes, indeed.'

'I am happy. For sometimes what we do is a mystery to those that are receiving the benefit and they will say: I am so tired or my body hurts or why is my mind not working and come to us in a way whereby they complain and are often angry because we have taken away their habitual method of interacting on the planet, whereas, you two seem to acknowledge it; granted you do not like it when you are tired, or, perhaps, feeling out of sorts, but you come back into alignment when you are with one another and when the channelling happens we can more easily capture that part of you which is out of alignment and straighten it. So, I am saying to you there is more to doing this channelling than just being aligned with a Guide and having your Higher Self connecting with you. That is a big part of it, but we want you also to know that many of your Guides are working with you at this time because you are so available and open and your hearts are expanded beyond belief when this happens.

So, we thank you, the elders thank you, you do not know them but they are out in your universe in a very contained space whereby no contrary energy can affect them. Their wisdom has been accumulating and growing and expanding for close to two million years. So, you will see that the Wise Ones, as they look upon you, and I do not say down upon you, because often times you are with them and interacting with them at night, receiving information as well. It is not always from the spaceships that you do receive your knowledge. The elders are very wise and are awakening you to your original ability. I say that as an originating being coming from that pool of souls when you and the Eternal Father decided it was time to be out and active in this universe. You were almost ejected from a womb-like atmosphere and you took on personality and commitment to do certain jobs, to be present, to be aligned to the energies on the planet and around the planet. Since that time which was approximately five million years ago, you have been coming and going and been learning. You have been tempted, have done things you needed to erase, other things that will lift you up to another alignment, an evolvement which has been going on thus and such for all these many, many years.

So, you can see that the knowledge that you have is not just knowledge being given to you from an outer source, we are awakening that knowledge that you have accumulated for many, many years. It is making it possible for you to be more aware and aligned with other aspects of your being that you have no idea of yet. Perhaps, it will come to be that when you are in the spaceships much of that will be revealed to you but there will still be treasures unbeknown to you that will become open and active as the planet is going into more turmoil.

You will stand strong, be one of the more valid leaders that we have on this planet and never need to think that your language or your inability to express yourself or whatever, will hold you back; you will burst forth, much as a chicken – a baby chick – would burst forth out of its shell. So, this is for you, my dear; your constancy, your light, your love – all the things that you are bringing onto this Earth are so exemplary that we want you to know what is happening for you shall be aligned to many of the Guides who are not visible. I do believe you have a question about the Crocus Group?'

'Yes, indeed.'

'Well, do not fear, you are certainly an integral part of the entities on this planet that they are working with and because you do like flowers and you do like gardening you are with the

191

elementals often, for this group works well with the divas and the elementals, the plant fairies and all those beings that you are unknowingly or, perhaps, sensing you are aligned with. Very often, they will come most to you when you least expect it. It seems like it is a paradox, but it is not for they will be there in the garden or when you are tending the birds or when you are just dreaming on your boat. You may expect them in the form of not being just one. You know what it is to have one Guide come in to your energy: is that correct?'

'Indeed.'

'Here you will have a group, most likely five, who will come and you will feel sparklers. They might have colour but more pronouncedly it will be light and you will see these light flashes ahead, on the side, behind, above, below – you may expect them anywhere – but when you notice it, you probably will rub your eyes saying I am seeing things. When it happens repeatedly and there will be little flashes of light, you will know the Crocus Group wants to tune into you. So, if it is at all possible, of course, if you are out in your boat and you are going towards a destination whereby you cannot sit and say: "Oh, I am open to you," they would understand. But we would like it, if possible, if you could come into the chapel or you could be in a space where you are comfortable and you know you will not be disturbed and say: "I am ready to receive the divine voice from the Crocus Group". You need to name them specifically and then, when they come, ask is this the Crocus Group and are you speaking the truth.'

'Thank you.'

'So, at all times, you will be aligned with them and let them speak first. It is best not to ask too many questions for they are still a bit timid about interacting with humans: they have been betrayed before. When there have been giant cataclysms upon this Earth, they came to try and stop it and prevent that which was the Atlantian dissolution. It happened in the Mayan civilisation. It has happened many times upon the Earth and these are the caring souls who have been constantly around the solar system. They are at different times on different planets or star systems, but they come at this time because your planet is going through something that has never happened to a celestial body before and they want to be sure that they have those beings who are also aligned to their way of thinking and can be ready to act when they are told something important. So, you will find this will be stepping up your energy, your capabilities, your pronouncements may be a word, but that word will carry ripples not just around the islands but around the planet. So, be expecting something very wonderful and monumental in the change that will happen. It will not influence your family life or how you interact with your family; they will always consider you as the same being you are but it is when you stand up in the name of this Crocus Group that you will become all powerful, such that you will not have known ever before in a lifetime.

Prepare yourself for it gently. You will ask your Guides what it is that you need to do or to stay aligned to, what energy is right for you at that time, so that they might say it is now and you will pronounce this word and if you begin to tremble or wonder how you, as a mortal, could do this then you will have a phrase or a word that will calm you and bring you back into your heart knowing that you are serving the Almighty Father from your heart space.'

'Thank you.'

'That is the principal message I wish to bring in today. If you have other questions?'

'A few, if that is okay?'

'Indeed.'

'Why is it we are both so tired?'

193

'There are stages when you are more tired or feeling more enlivened and we would say for Mary, last night, she was worked on considerably. Every part of her body was taken apart and re-aligned to this new energy so, if she is tired and feeling depressed today or, perhaps, not just the same, you might inform her that she has been re-organised. It is much as you would do with an aeroplane and take it in for a check-up and they take apart every bit, the motors are lying on the ground here, the tail section is over there and the fuselage is bare and wide open. So, she will undoubtedly feel not as well as she would normally like to feel and it might be advisable if she rests a great deal today and, perhaps, tomorrow she will have the same feeling but she is not to worry in any way that her problems will not be dealt with. She is trying to come to terms with it and we are very pleased that she is sorting it out in a very rational way, knowing that Spirit will handle her business managers, Spirit will handle her lawyer problems, Spirit will handle the betrayal that has gone on and that it will not allow this any longer to happen. It has gone on too often because she is a woman, because she has no allies to speak about on this planet until all of you came into her life. What they do not understand, these supposed enemies, though they do not realise they are being enemies, is that she is supported by Spirit as few other beings have ever been and it is a time to trust and to align herself constantly to her heart, to her light and to that Christ consciousness and grounding. There is no other way to be right now than totally at one with Spirit.'

'Thank you. I'm glad to hear that. What can we do to get closer to our Higher Self?'

'Excellent question. I praise you, the elders praise you, the Crocus Group are delighted for no group is here to take you away from that alignment to your Higher Self. It is and must always be your priority for, in aligning to your Higher Self, you are aligning yourself to the plethora of Guides. You are aligned to Skakus, you are aligned to Sananda, you are aligned to Mother Mary, you are aligned to St George – all of your Guides will come together in one magnificent applause to say: "Yes, you have climbed the ladder and you are there and you are connecting". They are almost plugging in the different sockets and whatever needs to sizzle will (if you will forgive the expression). It is a time when anyone who does that connecting from this third dimensional space and can fight the darkness and come through to being perfectly aligned with their Higher Self is being celebrated and honoured. Imagine twins who have been born identical and have been split up at birth; one goes one way and one goes the other way because of circumstances and their longing only will bring them back together as one entity, and, as they come together, can you see the light and the rainbows and the cheers and the excitement on our level? For we urge you and stir you and bring you to that point where you may be in that perfect alignment.

This is the highest thing that can happen for us: to see on an Earth space, on a third dimension which soon will disappear, but as you have conquered the darkness and come through it, you will be one of our major teachers to all those who will be spun into a fifth dimension and will have no idea where they are, what are the new rules, what are they supposed to look for or become. They will be totally lost so you will need to have had that experience to say: "We climbed the ladder, even in that density". Now that you are free of the density, we may tell you what the difference is and how you will feel because you are the "feeling" beings on this planet and we on our levels, are so far removed, we do not feel heat nor cold; we do not feel emotions as you do; we do not have that hunger gnawing at our interiors when we have not eaten. We do empathise with all the suffering that is going on on the Earth, but we cannot compare our feelings to your feelings as a group. When the planet does move into that fifth dimension, you will be there already as fifth dimensional beings and you will take on a group of this one or a group of that and you will know exactly where your talents will lead you.'

'Great. Thanks. Is it best to call them by name? If so, what are their names?'

'To whom do you refer? To the Crocus Group or to your Guides?'

'Yes, to our Guides, to Mary's Guides and my Guides.'

'Are you asking about your Guide from the Azores?'

'Yes, okay. This was the next one. Who was the Guide who came to me recently?'

'Does the word Emmanuel mean anything to you?'

'Yes.'

'And in the Azores, is he a Guide who is well known?'

'The son of the Holy Father.'

'And that is the one who is coming to you.'

'Thank you.'

'It is we who thank you. So you will know that you are in perfect alignment and if you have questions, if you have any worries, you are to open your heart to Emmanuel.'

'Thank you, thank you very much. I feel honoured. Do we need to cleanse the crystal?'

'No, it is doing very well as it is. There might be a fleeting energy that comes in but, as we have said before or others have said before me, these energies cannot stay, they are not comfortable and if there is a happening, it will just be a momentary happening and, unless it increases so that it becomes a daily event that something breaks or goes wrong,

196

there is no need to change the energy. You have done an excellent job in cleansing.'

'Thank you.'

'And we are indeed grateful for this is the home that you are working through and with and as you have captured that magnificence of it and brought it into the light, this is the very thing that we are wanting you to tell beings on this dimension about, that the light is not to be given to people as a natural gift, you will assume that the Sun is your natural gift but when it does not shine, then you will say to people it is up to each one of you to be that light, to create that light, to bring it in and to conquer the darkness. We are not going to do that for you and as each person takes on that responsibility of representing the light, fighting the darkness, letting that light shine through and break into the darkness, then you become closer to us and one of us eventually.'

'Beautiful, thank you. Could we invite an elderly gentleman to help us out?'

'He may be invited as a guest, but we would not suggest that he be relied upon as a steward; his heart is very fragile at this moment and if he added additional stress in wanting to do the best and to be ever present for everyone at all times, he might have an attack. We are hoping that as you and Mary step into that higher alignment, that you will be able to work with that heart energy around this gentleman and you, as well, may heal and do the work that would allow him to have that heart energy replaced and renewed for it is his heart that has been so broken by all the disappointments that he has had, but as he stays aligned, keep him busy with small tasks of woodcraft or repairing things or whatever he enjoys.'

'I will do that. Thank you very much.'

'Good. I'm glad you asked that question because that could have been a very, how could I say, debilitating mistake.'

'Thanks for being here this morning for us. It's an honour for us to have you here.'

'I am delighted being very comfortable, very welcomed and wanting to reassure you of all aspects, so, if there is any concern about what you do at night or how you use your skills that you know you are learning now with the space beings, I am very willing and happy to answer those questions. So, do you have more questions?'

'Now that you mention it, yes. Can you tell us what are we learning at night?'

'I was hoping you would ask. There is great mirth going on about you. You refrained from asking that which is, perhaps, dearest and nearest to you right now. It is a very valid question and now we are able to reveal it to you because the spaceships will be observed in the sky around the islands, perhaps at the end of May. In June they will start coming; people will view them, fleetingly. There will be a sign, for example, similar to the viewing of the spaceship above the water. Do you remember? It was just a shimmering bright light that did not move. That will be the way they first appear and then they will become discs that literally fly over the island and disappear very quickly. Next they will be seen in numbers, so much so that people will wonder what is happening, who are creating the turmoil. By September there will be landings, so you need to know that you will be one of their visitors and they will be taking you on their journeys. Visibly you will step into a spaceship and as they need the extra piloting ability, you may step up to the controls and will often be asked to take a needed journey to some part of the planet or you might go out into the universe. You have those skills. As you are learning with your boat, you are more qualified as a space pilot than you are aware. So, it is very valid information and you are at the stage

198

where your proficiency is such that you could do it tomorrow but they want to be sure that you may take trial runs, like semi-flight training in an aeronautics situation with changing temperatures. There may be failures of systems within that space that you will need to correct, things that will be done on a trial basis whereby there will be no fatalities, but you need to know how to get out of an emergency and make an emergency landing. We do not feel that you are needing the training yet of submerging into water, but it will come to be as you become more expert in what you do. Your skills are far advanced to those that are being given to the group. They will interact more with the crew of the ship and be able to ask questions. Mary is being given the same training that you have, so that people will not tend to say on planet Earth: "Oh look, there is again a man who has been chosen to do this work". You will stand up, both of you, and say we are both qualified and will step into your ships and give a demonstration if that is what is needed.

By September, the havoc and the violence will become very open. The islands will be shifting their energy out of that density of the third dimension into the fourth dimension. It does not mean you are yet fifth-dimensional beings but this is a self-enclosed energy system and, in great part thanks to you both, for as you have been working with the crystals, you have been allowing for the ships too; we say allowing and you may wonder at that, but you have been encouraging them. You are third dimensional, dense beings but you have raised and elevated your energy systems to such a level that you are interacting on many levels freely and openly with these space beings so that you are making it a welcome place for them to come to, and you are working with them. If they have a problem, you will deal with it during the day though you do not know how. That is why this self-contained unit out in the Atlantic ocean can be almost elevated to another dimension without you having to go through great trauma. It does not mean that the Earth shapes will change there. It is encircled by such an energy that you will feel as if you are in the fifth dimension although it will be only part of the fourth dimension.

199

The cruise ships will not be able to come in for they cannot sustain the energy. They are bringing in entities of different degrees of awakening; most of them are very dense and they would not feel at ease on these islands. Those who will come will be those who long for this energy, who come to be healed, who will come for the light and the love, the awakening; and it shall be that this island will be one of the major places where healing shall take place, but it needs to be safe and, for the moment, it is not safe. We will tell you when it is so and it will be merely a question of a telephone call saying we are starting a healing centre, would that be acceptable to government and governments will say: "We are delighted". So, you will work well with the hotels, the spas, all those who are representing healing and they need not know that you play such a pivotal role in all of this.

Do work with your Higher Selves in growing towards that wonderful happening. Thank your Higher Self for everything: the good, the bad, the light, the darkness, the hunger, the over-satisfaction of hunger; whatever it is you are feeling, thank your Higher Self with all your love. Imagine yourself hugging that Higher Self who is propelling you, spiralling you upward to a level that you have never known before in a physical body and as you keep that adoration and that love of your Higher Self, you will come to have revealing moments whereby you will see him or her as an angel or as a Light Being. You can picture it in many ways but you will be raising your own vibrations through that love and then that Higher Self can come down and join you and be one with you. You do not have to take a trip or go anywhere, it will come to be very shortly.'

'Thank you very much and I am really looking forward to it.'

'And we. So I leave you now with the blessing of the Holy Spirit and may all those Guides, those wondrous beings including the Crocus Group, the angels, the archangels, the Spirit Guides, all the different levels and dimensions that are

200

coming down to applaud this work, be with you and give you that peace that passes all understanding. In light and love I leave you with the blessings of the Holy Father. Amen.'

BE LIGHT. THE SPACE BROTHERS
ARE TEACHING YOU

Kuthumi

'How happy we are to be here. It's a moment of rejoicing and we wish just to be aligned to you and to do the bidding of our Holy Father.'

'Thank you.'

'Our first question today is to know if my friend and I are to work on anything and are we doing the right thing? Is there anything that you would suggest for us?'

'Be light and go with that wonderful light as you always have done and let no one hold back that wonderful energy that you are spreading. All the problems shall be solved if you just let us deal with it in a nice and pleasant way so no harm will be done to any human kind as you know so wisely; neither one of you wish to hurt anyone. At the same time do not let your spiritual Light Beings go dark and sink deeper and deeper. As you see trouble coming up ask for more guidance and help and be stronger. Fill yourself again with that wonderful light and wonderful energy that you are all very good at and surround yourself and say: "Dear Holy Father and wonderful Guardian Angels that surround me, light me up and help me through this wonderful day that you have provided for us." I pray with you and that light flows through you and may the wonderful energy go with you wherever you go. And make sure your troubles are dealt with in this spiritual way.'

'How wise and wonderful. Thank you Kuthumi. Is there something we need to know about the spaceships: I seem to be guided to ask you this morning?'

'As you get up – even when you sleep – you go up to the inside of the spaceship and you are manoeuvring around orbit; you are actually learning the wonderful techniques that have been a part of your knowledge for many, many years. It is just being refined. The Space Brothers need your help as well as your technical knowledge.

So, you are actually starting those new manoeuvres and the new techniques that they have developed and refined and by doing that the knowledge that you are receiving is so important at this moment that I do not explain exactly what you are going through because what has been planted in your Higher Self is for you to keep to yourself only and just keep your wonderful journeys as easy as possible and as light as could be. You do not have to force your light body to leave and to find a specific destination. As you relax and go to sleep your higher command says it's time to get up and go. Other than that just be patient. It's just like a child going to school and he wants to get his or her hands on that new toy of his or hers.

At the moment be careful and, as I speak right now, you probably feel the spaceship above you and this wonderful technology that we are using is being implanted in you.'

'Kuthumi: Is there something that will develop when we're out of the country whereby I can be of greater use and service to this planet?'

'Actually, that has already been happening to you and, yes, there you'll get more clarity about your mission and what you have been learning while you think that the human body sleeps. It will come to you and you will remember it. It's like

203

you can actually see the screen, you can see the wonderful colours and symbols, the buttons. Even the sky with its stars and galaxies will be clear for a while, you will be able to look into it and see the dangers and the directions you are going and you will remember them and you will pass those messages forward very clearly.'

'Will I grow closer to my Higher Self at that time?'

'At that time you will be in preparation, almost enlightened because that's what we are working on for all of you that are willing to give up this beautiful planet Earth and be implanted with the wonderful energy that our Holy Father has recommended for all human kind and it's, should I say – not an honour – but it's so wonderful to see a handful of humans actually getting together and saying: "I do this here and now for Love and Love only and for the love of the planet Earth and the Holy Father; that's all I am here for and I am ready for you any time you pick us up". If you knew how the angels sing and just flap their wings around all of you humans that are doing this wonderful work, it's beautiful to see them happy and to see that there are still some angels left on this planet you call Earth. So, by all means, enjoy yourself and be proud and every step you take by day say: "This is one step closer to my oneness with the Holy Father".'

'I don't know why, but I feel very tearful when you speak. It's an old longing; it's as if it's coming closer, the dream: the bringing of Heaven and Earth back together. Dear Kuthumi, I wanted to know if there is anything else I need to do, I feel different now; is there another alignment that is needing to be made?'

'Yes, dear one, and it's an honour for me to guide you this far as now that you are pure and clean it's so easy to give you good messages and at the same time, dear one, it's so easy for you to pick up bad influences. So, by all means, focus yourself that you are doing the right thing all the time and say: "The

204

work that I do, the first step that I take, everything I do are intentions of good only. I walk on the path of the Holy Father that I may do His divine work. I am that wonderful light that shines upon my forehead every time". Please follow through and don't let any destruction or any disturbance by any negative energy bother you. They will try and they will try to get in to you because they see now that you are pure and as that wonderful flower opens up, you see how many little flies try to get in before it's on its way. By all means keep shining and let no little fly put any disturbance in you. So, shine and feel the Sun, the warmth and the wonderful energy that you will always transfer. Walk in light and you will see the problems that they are trying to put on you will dissolve and melt away very easily.'

'Oh bless you, Kuthumi. You make it seem so easy and simple.'

'Well, dear one, it's an honour for myself and of all the little ones around here to have you both back and I will pray that you will come back – even if it is just to sit here and meditate a little bit – we will give you advice in silence. I pray that you all have a great, great day and that the Holy Father will always light up that wonderful path that you are beginning to see very wisely and fulfil yourself with love and light at all times. Amen.'

INTERACTING WITH THE ANGELS AND THE GALACTIC COMMAND

St Michael

'Good morning, my dears. I am St Michael and we know each other well. I come to you very often and am concerned about your well-being and how you do, how you are growing and how much we are interacting, you and me, along with the legions that work for me as well as the Galactic Command. I am seeing now that you are becoming very familiar with the ship, with the people on it, with the command, with those who are giving you instructions. It was not easy for you in the beginning because it was an unknown quantity for you and it was difficult to accept orders. You did not seem to want to comply with the rules, but may I congratulate you; you are being far more submissive and, may I say, trusting and that is an excellent sign; something that gives us courage and, how can I say, encouragement to know that you are not just accepting, but seeming to enjoy the space and realise that it is a home that you have known before.

Now, as you know, we are very active on many levels and are not always present on the fifth dimension so you might grow used to one of us and look for that individual – I may say brother or sister – when you arrive and not find them. So, if you could, we ask you to put that into your mind set not to be disappointed and open your inner eye and your dreams as to expecting a new experience each evening. We are not meaning to test you but it is the way we operate. So many of us are in demand and the turmoil is getting worse, as you know, on planet Earth, so, we are often called away at the last moment and cannot be there for what, perhaps, had been portrayed to you the night before that you would find thus and such and look for that kind of a space or person and you did not find them last night and you were disappointed – though that is not all the reason why you did not remember. So, let me not get ahead of my story and may I ask for your questions please?'

'Did we do the right thing with the crystal last night?'

'My dears, if I am to look a little bit like the mouse that has just been, I'm not saying caught, but has been cornered and is looking at who is the monster to trap him and finding out it is only the dog looking at him and he would say: "But what has that to do with us?". Well I was expecting a very monumental question and when I hear that I am cheerful, I am laughing, I am happy because I want you to know as you do not know and this is the charm of it: what the impact was of your actions, for it seemed like you were doing something very banal, very commonplace in following orders and reaching up and scooping out a piece of a crystal which could not be seen but that you knew was real. The fact that you held on to it with all of your strength and all of your concentration during the voyage and you arrived in the ship and declared that you had something very important to bring and you were shy, yet insistent as if you were coming from another world saying: "I have a piece of news from that other piece of the world".

Well, what it has developed into is a magnificent recording of an instance that was put into that crystal as part of its memory bank in the Atlantian times when all was not corrupt and exploding on that particular continent; but, there were wise priests who did know how to encode messages into crystals and that wise and beautiful crystal you have right next to you here knew that this piece was important and gave it up to you both. You received the coding instruments, Mary received the imprint or you could call it an x-ray, a blueprint; perhaps, the x-ray is the best description I can give to both of you right now because it's something that has left a message in between the lines whereby you would see the blues drawing the lines and something very similar to an architect's drawing, but it was there and we were able to capture it to take it off Mary by our very refined equipment. What we have discovered is a magnificent message. So, you will be the first to be informed of what it is that you carried so preciously and to know our gratitude will be perhaps a surprise for you tonight. So, we urge you please, both of you, come, be part of the festivities for, in truth, if you are not present, we cannot celebrate. I shall be there, as well, so look for me and look for my emissaries and all those who have been helping you throughout these past few months.'

'Thank you. Okay, well you've just explained what our schedule is for tonight. Can you explain what each of us did in the ship last night? Is there anything that we need to prepare or work on?'

'No, let me interrupt if I may – I am sorry to burst in here. I believe that in your preparation for tonight I would like you to be open and you can do that to open your third eye, to visualise whatever is there to try and capture the Light Beings, the frequencies to connect with what is, would you say, comfortable and what might not be comfortable. We want more impressions from you both as you are coming back because, do you see, the work that you are doing on the ship now is preparing you to welcome others, and you will be describing the journey to many on planet Earth as well as being on the ship to welcome them. The more you are observant of what is going on and what captures your attention, what is friendly, what is, perhaps, not so well known to you and might not even be in your mind set as familiar; we would like to know that by telling us you are familiarising yourselves with this phenomena, and the more observant you can be, the more delighted we shall be in knowing that your progress is advancing rapidly.'

'Thank you. Do I need to do any more painting at home tonight?'

'It would be advisable. Sometimes when you think you have cleaned the house and you leave it for a day or two, the dust comes back and some unwanted critters come in through the door, but this looks to us as if it is relatively clean; I think it would not hurt to do the usual ritual – I would say for at least three to four more days until you are totally comfortable that it is all as you have prepared it, that the light is of the same intensity, that the walls are at the distance you have set them at and that it feels clean. You might even ask your Guides before leaving: "Is everything in order or do I need to work on the walls?"'

'Thank you. Does Mary need to be back in the ship tonight to be worked on?'

'Well, if this is a disease I'm sure it needs a new name but she has accurately pinpointed it. Of course, and she understands now why much of her body is aching. For example, the lungs; at times they feel like they are collapsing inside even though it is not the case. It is because you are becoming accustomed to breathing a different air and that requires a different manipulation of the lungs. They are, how can I say, "coded", if that again is not overusing an expression, but they have been programmed to do a different function for you. The air that you breathe within the spaceship is different and though you are in your light bodies and not relating to it in this body, you do carry it down from that experience so that your lungs are beginning to work in a different fashion. So, if the diaphragm, the lungs – even the heart area – is feeling a bit painful, you will know that it is because of the air and the quality and the way in which you need to breathe within the ship that is impacting on that. It will not affect your health. Normally, you ought to be able to carry on as you have done previously.'

'Thank you. Is it appropriate that Mary goes on studying?'

'It is a good question and we are very thankful that you have asked it. Some of it is very appropriate and some of it is not, so I would advise Mary to ask her Guides to be present and to please inform her as to which chapters she needs to read. Others might tend to confuse her and to interrupt the process she is on because she needs to stay focused. She needs to direct her attention to us, to the spaceships and not be diverted by other stories of past events. Now is the time to focus on the present and on where you both are. I say this for both of you, where are you now, where are you going to be tomorrow? That you will know when you wake up in the morning what the experiences are that you are having. I wish you to live in this kind of a story rather than a paperback book that is feeding your mind.

You see, your sensory equipment which means your emotional body, your mental body, your light body, all your subtle bodies are ingesting this information in different parts and in different ways so that you might not feel very well the next day which means that your bodies are very active. Imagine being given a huge feast where all kinds of food are being offered to you and you partake of all of it, and you swallow it, and your poor digestive system is saying: "Help, we don't know what to do with all these strange exotic foods. Which places do they belong in?" Well, this is something that is happening to both of you.

May I give an answer now to a question Mary had earlier but has not been put in your list and that has to do with those who are coming to the island as guests. I wish you to sit down and meditate very carefully as to who should be introduced to the crystals and to the passageway to the ship and who may not for this could be devastating if certain ones succeed, come back, explain where they have been, what it was like and what was your experience like and one sits in a corner looking very glum because he or she did not manage to go up. Now we will need to work on all of them as they come in and we will ask them to be out around the crystal, to be talking to the crystal, to go in and lie down on the floor somewhere – perhaps the round room which you have all known before – and to try to release

210

your subtle bodies – in other words your light body to get it out. Do you see, you two succeeded in this very quickly; it is an art that you know and you have understood and you had a purpose where to go so you knew exactly what to do. Now, the others have not practised this and some are good at it and others are not so good at it.

So, we do want to caution you that it is not just a welcome; we have a surprise for you and we are all going up in this wonderful passage and some will look very confused and work it out with discernment and prayer – especially at night. You might ask who is properly prepared and who is not and you might do an exercise whereby everyone can interact in some way but those who are gifted will still have the experience and those who have not succeeded in that particular experience will succeed in another so they will not feel that they are lesser than.'

'Thank you. Why did my friend not remember what happened last night? Is there anything special that we need to concentrate on while in the ship?'

'That again brings me back to my original topic of being more open, to expecting anything and knowing that you are given the assignment of remembering as much as you can. You see, it was at the point where you offered your gift. It was what you had expected in your mind set, but once you had given it, then you were taken to a place that was totally unfamiliar, unexpected and you were almost overwhelmed by the event. So, you chose not to remember because it was not something you had looked forward to and that was living up to your expectations at that point. It is not a mistake – mind you anything that happens to you on the ship is not a mistake – it is therefore a purpose because many whom you will be guiding and teaching will have the same problems as you so these human foibles that are common to every human on this planet will surface at some point or other; some that you have never even thought of doing or daring, such as screaming and hysteria because you find it very strange. We would not do

211

that nor would Mary but the time will come when others will also blank out. They don't like what they see and this isn't familiar and it isn't what they had expected so they are not going to participate.

We want you to be as open as you can; know that what you are experiencing are things you will talk about and you will tell people about and, in as much as you can, we would appreciate it if you would remember as many details – even a light or a face or a room. You do that very well: remembering to describe a room and the space you were in – whatever you can – if you can note it in a book in the morning, first thing when you wake up so you do not lose it. You did have impressions this early morning, but with rushing about and getting ready they were lost – temporarily speaking. I think you will be reminded tonight; it will not be the same experience but I believe you will be more open.'

'Thank you. I will prepare myself for that.'

'Excellent.'

'Why are we feeling unsettled today?'

'Well, it's partially about expectations but it is also about the change of weather and you need to be attentive to that because while you are working, you are getting warm and then you tend to take your jacket off and forget that it's no longer summer so I would suggest that you come with an extra layer tomorrow and do take some vitamins or whatever you need to help you tonight because the microbes are in the air and you might be susceptible. We would not like to see you become ill right now because you are in a tremendous growth period and, as you expand and grow, you are absorbing worlds of information. You are going as fast as any humans have ever gone in a process so we encourage you through this: all the struggles and the difficulties or whatever you might have when you come back into your body. You need to be very cautious and very careful with it and do take a warm bath tonight or whatever to

212

get comfortable again and stay warm – even a cloth around your throat if it begins to bother you and never mind what anyone says.

We are encouraging you, please, to look after yourself because this is a period that you have available to you and once the house guests have arrived, you will not have that leisure to be able to go at ease, go and come, be with the crystal – the pace will be different. So, it is going to be more intense, they will want to know much, they will be pulling energy from you whereas now you have the energy; you are getting it from the ground, the soil, the crystal, the connection with the ship overhead and we do want you to continue to grow and expand – you might even be gone by the time these guests arrive at which point you and Mary will be laughing on some other dimension and encouraging your walk-in substitutes to do your job for you.'

'Thank you. I'm looking forward to seeing you tonight.'

'Well, I have a point to make again: do not neglect your crystal. It is too cold for you tonight to go out and greet it but I would suggest before you do join in the column of light that goes over it. If you would talk to the crystal it will be aware of your presence; bring as a gift as much light as you can and love and thank it, and tell it what benefits its gift has been to the world at large, to the fifth dimension – to many dimensions. It is giving us another understanding of what this planet Earth has been programmed to establish throughout the entire universe and it is going to be more helpful than any kind of readings that we could do for any of you, so, please, thank the crystal. Give it your love, hug it, whatever you can do to show it your gratitude and that would be very, very helpful – for us as well, thank it on our behalf.'

'Thank you.'

'And I thank you and I look forward to finding you one of these evenings at home.'

213

* * *

'Good evening, dear ones. What an auspicious occasion.'

'Thank you. You are Kuthumi? Thank you for coming to us, I was hoping it would be you. There is quite a strong energy in here this evening. Is there something special happening?'

'Somebody else is here with us. Yes, dear one, and he will probably take over from me after a while. So, go ahead dear one, I will let you know when the time is up.'

'Thank you. What I wanted to ask was that I just went to ask the crystal if there was a message we could bring in tonight and I interpret it as saying that there is a wave coming towards us from the Pleiades in approximately three weeks' time that is meant to destroy us. Is that accurate?'

'That is their purpose, but at that time – before that actually happens – both of you and others will be ready to fight it and the way you are going to fight it is so wonderful and light that the dark side cannot penetrate. Their main fear is of you graduating from planet Earth and taking your wonderful secrets that have been taught here and sharing them with us and others above and lightening up the spaceships which would make the voltage a lot easier to destroy them; hence they are fighting back. Since you have the knowledge already in hand of what to do with it, I will let you speak with our Holy Father when the time comes for that, and I will leave when you are ready to answer that, but there are a few other things I am sure you wish to speak with me about so, if you don't mind leaving that for the last question He will come down and send his lights and will talk to you.'

'Thank you very much Kuthumi. The last question was what did we learn last night and is there anything we need to know for tonight when visiting our friends?'

214

'Yes, dear one. See how easy it is when you ask and at the same time how easy it is and joyful when you wonderful children do as you are taught so heartily, so wonderfully and so bravely. I admire you, particularly, dear Mary. You actually pulled your friend out of the cobwebs and well done, even when he is still not quite clear about what's going on some of the time; but, he will get it thanks to you – keep pushing him along.

And, yes, what you will work on tonight will be in a similar way almost where they left off from last night. They will carry on with the wonderful work they are doing with you and are teaching and, at the same time, tell your friend not to expect so much; just to be there for them and be there with his love as he has been but not to expect so much. He will see more that way by being so strong and so willing to learn and co-operate whereas, when that strong side of him dominates, he will just blind his third eye because his ego is taking over. So, my dear one, ask him just to be there with his love and be surrounded by that wonderful energy around him and he will be able to enjoy and see everything.'

'That's beautiful Kuthumi. I got into a rather emotional – how can I put it – "drama" the other night and I am almost ashamed of myself because that's not like me.'

'Dear one, the people you are going to work with, they are going to come up with exactly the same problems and you are learning how to deal with that and you will go out there in a completely different mood tonight. You should come back optimistic and I would love to hear from you tomorrow.'

'Is that optimistic or up to mischief?!'

'Optimistic.'

'Thank you very much. I look forward to it very much and I did remember a bit but, I think I lost consciousness of what was going on at some point because my friend tells me when he comes back and if we are gone that long then something certainly must have been going on that I don't remember.'

'That's like a robot – they put the microchips in you and they are programming you and those memories will come through very wisely. It's like coming from a tape recorder, if you like, and it will be very, very clear to you.'

'Excellent and I pray that I may thank them and some day thank you personally.'

'And they thank you for the wonderful energy that you both bring up at the same time and thanks again for the vortex and the wonderful crystal that you all did so well to preserve and bring up to their hands. I thank you.'

'Is the crystal in any danger?'

'Not as long as you both are there to protect it and it will protect you – it's like teamwork, if you like to call it. As long as you love that crystal, the same love goes for both of you and others. That energy will be a lot stronger and no one can get in between that wonderful love bond that you have all created.'

'Beautiful. Thank you Kuthumi. I have no more questions.'

'Then, dear one, I may go and I invite now one of my dearest, dearest advisers who has been waiting very patiently, watching and observing, to come in. If you wouldn't mind just waiting a few seconds please.'

'Thank you.'

* * *

'Good day.'

'Thank you for being so patient and waiting for me. Yes, dear ones, have no fear and I would love to see you both after this wonderful session going up to the crystal and just saying: "Dear one, we hold our Holy Father in our holy hands and we always will be together no matter what; we will fight any energy and any black holes that come towards us; we will fight in the love of our Holy Father and at all times we will be joined together as the light of the Sun shines on the planet Earth and as the Earth rotates and becomes dark and when the light is shining somewhere else.

Is it possible then that darkness one day may block the whole planet? Yes, they are trying. By you wonderful Light Beings opening the vortex as you have done, that has been a way to get not only the light to shine here forever but, also, to help you communicate with the human Light Beings very easily. So, as you go on your wonderful journeys at night, ask for the Holy Father to be with you at all times, even when you get up to the inside of that majestic ship, that you are there having fun and learning wisely but still open your heart and let that beautiful light come down and warm it up, as the Sun warms you as you sit by it, and if you ever feel a breeze blowing and then become cold, by all means, open up your heart and let that Sun shine again and say: "Dear Father, I work for you and you only. Guide me by your wonderful light and heart and let no negative energy or thoughts pass by me; as they come by this wonderful reflection – like a mirror – it shines back to them and this wonderful light will go further and further and push them back to where they came from and let a different light shine upon them, take them out of that dark hole and raise them up as far as you can with one hand only, dear one, and the other one to make sure that they don't come near you". Raise them up with your left hand if you wish and with your right hand just push that wonderful light and give it to our Holy Father and say: "Holy One, now it is in your hands. Could you please take care of it and let your wonderful light shine again on us forever and ever. We are here to work with you, dear one, and only you we obey". I pray to you to do this in the name of our Holy Father and, I beg you, feel the little

217

children, the innocent children, of the wise ones and, as you are that little child, and at the same time you are the eyes of wisdom from above. Let it shine. Yes, be innocent as that little child, but as wise as the Holy One above and you will always carry that with you just by asking and doing as you have always done. I pray for you, dear ones: please go in harmony and I thank you for being so wise and listening so carefully. Adonai.'